Always Look Back

A Jewish Combat Infantryman's Memoir

Always Look Back

*A Jewish Combat Infantryman's
Memoir*

Alvin A. Hanish

VANTAGE PRESS
New York

. FIRST EDITION

Published by Vantage Press, Inc.
516 West 34th Street, New York, New York 10001

Manufactured in the United States of America
ISBN: 0-533-14089-7

Library of Congress Catalog Card No.: 01-130962

0 9 8 7 6 5 4 3 2 1

Time, Life, and Death
Are the Measures of All Things (A.H.)

To all Those with:
Laughter on Their Lips,
Tears in Their Eyes,
And Grief in Their Hearts

Contents

Always Look Back

A Jewish Combat Infantryman's Memoir

I

On Pass to Paris

"Hanish, I am giving you a six-day pass to Paris, and with that, a package of condoms. I expect you to use them. If you don't, you won't get anther pass from me." This came from First Sgt. Ginelli of our Co. A, 415th Infantry Regt., First Battalion, 104th Infantry Division, commanded by General Terry Allen, one of the best.

"I'll do my best," I replied. (Not for me. I had other more practical uses for the condoms—like waterproofing any of the small items that I wanted to keep from getting wet, e.g., extra socks, pens, handkerchief, tissue, etc.)

"Report tomorrow morning at 0900 in front of the C.P. with a fully packed duffel bag. Leave your military gear behind. Also draw some K-rations. There will be a truck waiting with some other men." I thanked the sergeant, bid him goodbye, and left his office. I considered myself very fortunate. After all that I had gone through, I had found a real friend in First Sgt. Ginelli; an Italian from Chicago. I found most Italians the friendliest of them all.

I was very thankful for this six-day pass to Paris, not only because I needed the rest and change from the fatigue and horrendous experiences of combat, but also for a chance to meet with my younger brother, who in his last letter to me a month ago, gave me the address of his outfit (driving the Red Ball Express supply trucks), which was stationed a few miles outside of Paris.

Company A had earned a rest and was placed in reserve near the banks of the Rhine, Cologne, March 1945. Our company, as well as our whole division (whatever was left of it) had participated in three major campaigns from their inception in Holland (October 1944), "Spearheading the thrusts to drive the Germans out of the towns and cities west of Cologne." I was one of the few of the original complement formed in Camp Carson, Colorado, who had survived, including First Sg. Ginelli. The others were casualties of one type or other—killed, wounded, taken prisoner, victims of various psycho-traumas, blinded, loss of various members of the body, and a few of the guys who chose to run off the field of battle, never to be heard from again. (What happened to them anyway?) Our company had already turned over two and a half times. So far there were over 300 dead.

The next morning, I reported as instructed with a loaded duffel bag drawn from supply, which included my trusty Kodak box camera with 620 film. I had brought it from the States, and never used it in Europe. I expected to have ample time in Paris.

When I got to the one-and-a-half-ton troop carrier truck, I found some fellows already seated on the inside on the sides. I tossed my duffel bag on to the aisle between the seated men and hopped in. There were four men seated on the wooden slats on one side, and three men seated across, which left one spot for me near the tailgate, looking out on the left side over my right shoulder. I greeted them, but I knew none of them. There had been so many men who had joined us from the Replacement Depots (we called them "Repot Depots") that there was hardly any time to really get acquainted. They were generally nice guys, and we managed to establish an easy rapport with each other. They were unlike the group I first met when I attached to the division back in the States. Most of those men were now gone.

The truck was covered overhead with a canvas canopy much like the covered wagons of yore. The driver was a Tech. Sgt. and his companion was a corporal. He came to the back of the truck, raised the hanging tailgate, and bolted it to the sides of the truck. He returned to the front, and we started on a memorable trip with exhilarating anticipation of spending time in "Gay Paree." Imagine a free trip to Paris at government expense!

The tailgate came only halfway up, leaving in air and looking out on the "magnificent" passing scenes of neglected fields, homeless people; shabbily dressed humanity moving along the highway by foot, by horse and cart, by makeshift carriages and by trying to hold each other up as they moved along. It was a sorrowful sight.

I did not know these fellows, as I mentioned before. The four seated across were in animated discussion with each other, evidently buddies from the depot. The three alongside me were doing the same, also quite obviously buddies. I felt alone. I missed Shraeder, with whom I had struck up quite a friendship in Camp Carson. We had very much in common. We were both ASTP. What happened to him after we landed in France is quite a story to be told later.

2

I can only say at this time that he was well versed in the Gilbert and Sullivan plays with their lyrics and songs which he applied to the convolutions of the military commands, plans, programs, and administrative foul ups at Camp Carson. His recitations at unexpected moments showed an uncanny perceptive awareness of what was going on about him. I enjoyed them immensely.

At times, he would appear in the doorway leading into our barracks at Camp Carson, a rather burly, middle-sized figure, with leggings that would reach up to his knees, which forced the upper trousers around his thighs to "bloom out." His shirts always appeared oversized so that he appeared hardly as "The Very Model of a Modern Major General," a song he often sang. At the very beginning of his recitations, as he appeared in the doorway, he led off with one from *HMS Pinafore,* viz:

When I was a lad I served a term
As the office boy to an attorney's firm
I cleaned the windows and swept the floor,
And polished up the handle of the big front door.
I polished up the handle so carefully
That now I am the ruler of the Queen's Navee.

(Additional stanzas would be aired as befitting the circumstances.)

So, I was more or less by myself. My thoughts receded into the past, recalling the events that led up to the war, and to my wonder how I came to be riding in this military troop carrier with a bunch of guys I barely knew, on the way to Paris.

Events moved swiftly in those times, and one becomes aware that one is not the captain of his fate. As man proposes, it is not always God that disposes, but that man also disposes. We are all like pawns on a giant chess board, being shuffled hither and yon by master chess players and their cohorts and advisors, and not to mention least of all, the vagaries of God's world of natural disasters.

In this vein, I recall that on graduating from high school in the spring of 1930, in which I had attained an overall high grade of 95, and an Arista Honor as well, which led to my being accepted to the free college of the City of New York. I intended to obtain a bachelor's degree with the hope of improving my employment prospects for a steady, decent, well-paying job. My father was a carpenter, having learned his trade as a young boy in Russia before coming to America as a young man—narrowly managing to

3

escape as a soldier with the help of his older brother, from the repeated savage pogroms, perpetuated by the Cossacks against Jews. But as the Depression set in after the stock market crash of 1929, my father's employment became sporadic, sometimes good, sometimes bad. It was always subject to the declining pace of home building, to the whims of the "Union Business Agent," and to the changes in weather conditions, all of which drove my mother crazy with five children to care for. I intended to enter Federal Government Service, which would at least assure me steady employment.

I entered City College in September 1930 as part of the class of 1934, but had to drop out after one year of studies in 1931. One year after the stock market crash of 1929, banks closed and factories shut down. Unemployment became rampant. Money became scarce. The deep, dark, anxiety-ridden Depression followed. Demoralization set in. I was ready to take any kind of job, no matter how menial, just to survive and to help my father pay the rent. The conditions in the United States during the depression are well-documented. No sense in going over that, except to mention that I, as well as others, took any job paying anywhere from five to eight dollars a week, working ten hours per day, including Saturdays. I wish to mention that I was a Jewish youngster from Brownsville, Brooklyn; densely populated by Jews doing their best to survive and to at least pay their rent, having lost all of their bank savings.

The pernicious propaganda floated through newspapers and the radio against Jews was a canard of the worst sort of anti-Semitism by Christians (Father Coughlin and Charles Lindbergh) in their preaching of the "perfidious" practices of Jews to scheme, to rob, to control international finances, and to influence the United States Government. And here I was from the Jewish ghetto of Brownsville where I and others were scrounging around to earn nickels and dimes to buy some food to survive. What gall!

If economic and social conditions were not bad enough, the effects of these conditions were manifested in the horrors that were breaking out all over the globe.

In the Far East, Japan was ravaging Manchuria and China, killing, bombing, maiming, torturing, enslaving, and raping. In essence, committing the most barbarous acts, comparable to those perpetrated by the peoples of the ancient pagan world and that of the Middle Ages (Christian Crusades), including the invasions of the barbarians from the third to seventh centuries into western Europe. It was in this climate of misery and unemployment when people were selling apples on the streets for five cents

4

apiece in order to stay alive, that Marxist ideological fringe groups sprang up, each proclaiming that they had found "the scientific socialism to Nirvana." I decided to study for a bachelor's degree in social science—commonly referred to by science students as "crap courses." I was not ready to give allegiance to any of these half-baked, mushy-minded, convoluted, distorted notions of the causes and cures of the social and economic collapse of the capitalist system.

I became knowledgeable of all of these groups of firebrand "revolutionaries" as they set up their stands on the corners of the main street in Brownsville, spewing forth their programs and divine insights that made not the slightest bit of sense. They were on the corners each night—the Lovestoneites, the Browderites, the Trotskyites, the Stalinists, the anti-Stalinists, the socialists, the I.W.W.ites, and the general run of pseudo-hyped-up left-wing intellectuals, and of course, the Contras, who opposed everything and everyone. Incredulous! It must be understood, however, that these groups represented no more than about 5 percent of our community. Most people paid not the slightest bit of attention to them.

There were similar acts of barbarism—not as bad as in the Far East, preached under the ideological doctrine of the "Dictatorship of the Proletariat" advocated by the founder of "Scientific Socialism" (Communism), Karl Marx. His half-baked theories of "Class Struggle" and exploitation of the masses engendered by private property ("ownership of the means of production") enunciated in *Das Kapital* and in his *Political Economy,* and calling on the proletariat to throw off "the shackles of enslavement," takeover the government for the purpose of establishing a classless society. It is incredulous that pseudo-leftist intellectuals would embrace this nonsense of a society. . . . I met them in the alcoves of City College when there was no such thing as a "classless" society. Social classes are essentially socio-statistical entities. We tend to group individuals according to similarities in ideas, status, roles, wealth, or lack of it, power, influence, employment, material relationships, ownership of property, etc. Social classes are essentially amorphous entities, without a head. They assert themselves politically, in writings, gatherings, conferences, and declarations of agreement for action, influence, and change. The allegiances of individuals are usually "fluid" in practice as they tend to move from one class to another. The allegiance for the moment will depend on whatever advantage or profit to be gained for them.

As it turned out, these pseudo-Marxists had not the slightest idea of what it was all about, and what was worse for all of us, as their movements spread throughout the United States, their writings, their massive assemblages, their implied threats to the very cornerstone of the Constitution of the United States with its guarantees of freedom, ownership of private property, of life and law, engendered the emergence of fascist-minded reactionaries. Under these conditions, sympathy and support for Hitler and his gang of cutthroat hoodlums, together with Mussolini and his upperclass cohorts, were embraced by the rich, the propertied classes, the religious groups, the southern racists, and even Christian poor.

In between, the Jews were "thrown to the dogs" (so to speak) and painted as perfidious creatures not only anti-Christ, but responsible for his death. Pope Pius XII, without ever raising the cross in their defense, did nothing more than signing a concordant with Hitler—*quid pro quo*—don't bother me. I won't bother you. And so was sewn the cataclysmic upheavals of suffering, death, destruction, murder, looting, and theft as that megalomaniac stormed throughout Western and Eastern Europe, a regression to ancient Roman times.

It did nothing for these supporters and sympathizers who thought he would destroy Stalin. Hitler turned on them also. None of these doctrines had any basis in fact. In applying these mental aberrations in practice (by government), millions and millions of people of all ages were victims of the most outrageous acts of murder, senseless killings, torture, confiscation of property, humiliation, and worst of all, genocide (of the German type—"blood"—and also of the Russian Marxist type—class.) All in all, for the "Glory of the IDEA." (*This is for you, Karl.*) Instead of "Dialectical Materialism," it would be more correct to preach "Dialectical Ideo-Materialism." This would show the interaction of "IDEA and the Material," aspects of human activity which becomes the "Demiurgus of new social and economic forms and development." (*Please note: Demiurgus, in Philosophy, is defined as the creator or fashioner of the world.*)

Nothing much was said except by some newspapers and columnists (Dorothy Thompson, for one) and an occasional outpouring of outrage by Winston Churchill and President Roosevelt and other government officials—except for the Waspish State Department, which considered all this as the usual wartime propaganda. As for the Catholic Church in Rome, nothing much was heard except for an occasional squeak out of Pope Pius XII. Had the Pope, as the vicar of God and Jesus Christ, put his golden official vestments aside and donned a robe of sackcloth, raised the cross as he strove over the rock cliffs of the Apennines and the French Alps, followed by his retinue of Cardinals, similarly dressed, and each also carrying the cross, into France and across to the German border to confront Hitler's juggernaut, perhaps this would have put an end to this horrific conflagration of killings and destruction of our civilization. This, of course, would be too much to expect. The Pope, as usual, in error, decided to sign a concordat with Hitler in the hope of saving the Catholic Church.

As for the dialectics of blood, it is hardly worth the trouble to comment upon. Blood has nothing to do with culture, behavior, thought, individual characteristics, nor the "superiority of the Aryan Race." The Jews are not members of a race. Jews are members of a culture that developed over centuries, cemented by the worship of the "God" Jehovah, and of the divinely conceived Old Testament. The very same "God" was hijacked by the Christians and Moslems and made their own.

Aryan, from the Sanskrit *Arya*, meaning noble, denoted a people in prehistoric time settled in Iran and India. Their language noted Aryan was of Indo-European beginnings, and used only in regard to the language. During the nineteenth century, there arose a notion propagated most assiduously by Comte DeGobineau and later, by his disciple, Horton Stewart Chamberlain, of an Aryan race. Those who spoke Indo-European languages, who were considered to be responsible for all the progress that mankind had made and who were also morally superior to Semites, Yellows, and Blacks, and of the government policy of exterminating Jews, Gypsies and other non-Aryans (*Encyclopedia Britannica*).

The Aryan race of Germany was a mixture of rape, intermarriages, Slavs, Vandals, Goths, Vikings, Scandinavians, Jews, Huns, Teutons, and what have you. So Karl, your theories on social-class confrontations as the cause of human misery, and the promise of establishing a classless society in Russia by Lenin and Stalin, would undoubtedly end in disaster, not only for the Russian people, but also for the rest of the world. They will find that the theories could not solve the problems that human society faced each day because they were based on false premises.

Marxism, as formulated in practice, was also responsible for the initiation of terror not only in Russia, but also throughout the globe. It was Lenin, the architect of the Russian Bolshevik Revolution, who wrote a tract advocating the use of terror to destabilize capitalist governments. This was taken up by Stalin as a state policy not only in Russia, but in support of revolutionary groups in other countries. A copy was made by Hitler and his gang of murderers. It kept him in power until his death in 1953. With terror, Stalin dictated the thoughts and behavior and the allegiance of all segments of the Russian population. With the use of terror, he eliminated all opposition and difference of opinion reflected by the very supporters who helped him reach the supreme Soviet power of the Secretary General of the Communist Party. Most of them were eventually tried as enemies of the party and of the people, and were summarily shot. Trotsky, who was his main opponent, and who was chosen to supplant Stalin by Lenin before Lenin's death, fled Russia for his life. Trotsky ended up in Mexico where he was also "done in" by an ax cleaving his skull. So much for the splendors of dictatorship of the proletariat.

So, Fascism arose in deadly opposition. The rest is history of which we were all a part. Hitler learned from the Bolshevik masters how to attain power and to keep it by the use of terror, deception, and distortion of historical facts. Fascism was the blood cousin of Communism.

At last the truck stopped. The sergeant announced a rest stop for "relief." It was slow going. We all got off, found a spot off the road and did our thing. We walked about a bit to stretch our legs. We found a relaxing spot against a tree, took out a K-ration, which we carried in our jacket pockets, and proceeded to eat the contents. We drank water from our canteens, chatted as we smoked our cigarettes.

When done, we went back to the truck, hopped on, took our seats for the remainder of the trip to Rheims, France, our stop for the night. Some slept, some talked. Some just remained silent in thought. I chose to pull out memories of my entry into service, and therefore of my adventures, misadventures, and survival in the infantry and combat. So the story unfolds.

II
Initial Steps Towards the Military

I was drafted into the military service in June 1942 from Washington, D.C., where I was employed by the FSA (Federal Security Agency) as a statistical clerk. On December 7, 1941, when Pearl Harbor was attacked by the Japanese, I was staying at Mrs. T's boarding house in the second alphabet area of Washington, D.C. with a group of fellows and girls, all Jewish, also working for the federal government. Working for the government then was about the only decent job one could get. It paid fairly well and it was steady. Mrs. T was a Jewish woman, very friendly, who offered two meals a day at a very reasonable monthly rate, room-sharing for two.

We all came from different parts of the country, and it was very interesting to meet Jewish fellows and girls, whose parents more or less came from different parts of Eastern Europe. We were all first-generation Americans, and to some extent, we shared many attitudes and background of the households into which we were born.

I make mention of all this because I have no other way of explaining and clarifying my thoughts and experiences except to mention (as per Philosophy 101) that I moved from one universe of discourse to another, e.g. from college to employment in Washington, D.C.; from family to marriage; to the army from government employment, where I had to adjust to a new universe of discourse. The suddenness of all this stretched my psyche a bit. I managed to adjust especially to army and combat life.

So to start again, I was drafted the second time (the first one did not take) in June 1942, and I was sent to Camp Lee, Virginia for basic training, a God-forsaken place of excessive heat and humidity, one step above hell. There I was submitted to a battery of I.Q. and aptitude tests that were necessary to place me in some category of abilities and education. My I.Q. rating turned out to be about 130, somewhat above average. My MOS (Military Organization Status) designation was for administrative-clerical functions. Each morning, I had basic military training, and in the afternoon, I reported to the Long House where about 150 of us took typing lessons.

The instructor stood on a podium and shouted out the instructions as indicated in the book of exercise lessons we had alongside the typewriter. As much as I tried, I found it difficult to coordinate my fingers with my visual perceptions. The instructor, with his uncanny, imperceptible awareness, became conscious of my faulted propensity to hit the wrong keys. From the podium came a torrent of indescribable verbiage that resembled the clatter and clang of falling metal pots and pans. This continued for several days, until one day, on returning to the barracks, I found posted on the bulletin board a notice for openings in K-9 Corps (dog-training) for volunteers. With unaccustomed alacrity which belied the stupor that one is enshrouded in in military basic training, I hot-footed over to the Administrative Office and asked that my name be placed among those honored volunteers. I wrote to my wife to inform her of this daring, risky step I was taking into the unknown. She replied, as befitting a good wife, that I was really going to the dogs and to damnation to boot. I should have known that no one in his right mind volunteers in the army for anything. This was a commonly held belief. *Woe is me!*

It did not matter to me. I had to get away from the clatter of those typewriters and that off-beat howling that came from the podium. A week later, I was called to appear at a certain room near the office, where I came before three seated men, two officers (a colonel and psychologist and a civilian dog trainer). I was asked:

Q. Do you like dogs?
A. Yes.
Q. Did you ever have a dog
A. Yes. (I really did. A spitz.)
Q. Do you think you have the patience and ability to train dogs that may be difficult?
A. Yes.

"OK, stand on your right foot, move your eyes from right to left as you lift your right arm in the air, swinging it in circles."

Which I did. This was repeated with the left foot. The colonel then leaned forward on the desk with the right arm, elbow bent, holding a lead pencil in his right hand.

"Now," he said, "I am going to move this pencil from side to side, and

10

I want you to follow it only using your eyes. At the same time, I want you to swing both arms from the side of your thighs, touching your fingers of both hands above your head."

I did this.

"OK, you will be notified in due time."

I had not the slightest notion of what I did, but I figured I was in.

III

The K-9 Corps

Two weeks later, I was called into the Administrative Office, and I was told to draw new clothing allowances with a duffel bag from supply. I was given my travel orders and money allowance. The next day, I found myself on a one-and-a-half ton troop carrier truck heading for Fort Royal, Virginia, Remount Station (horses) in the Blue Ridge Mountains. There were two other trucks coming along. All together, there were about twenty five men in all. It did not take long to get to Fort Royal. It was evening as we ascended the hill to the station. We were greeted with a horrendous, ear-shattering outpouring of dogs howling, barking, whining, squealing that filled the night air. It seemed that we had passed the dog kennels. The men in the truck looked at each other and wondered how it would be possible to sleep, much less get used to it. We did.

As we drove into the camp, we were each assigned to a tent that was set upon a wooden platform. Inside there were five army canvas cots (not the home kind) placed around the tent with wooden storage chests at the foot. In the middle, there was a pot-belly stove with a chimney tube rising to the top through a hole in the tent to the outside air. Pieces of chopped wood were placed on the side of the stove, which we had to replace as it was used up. We had settled in. We had a meal in the mess hall.

It did not take long to get used to this life. It was comfortable and warm on the inside. Outside the forest air was cool, dry, and fresh, not like the insufferable hot, humid, foul air of Camp Lee, Virginia.

It was October, 1942. There were forests about us, which I like. It was very country like. We all felt free and loose. Military discipline was at a minimum, and we went about our duties without overbearing restraint so characteristic of a military camp.

There was the Long House, which held the facilities for cooking, kitchen, tables and benches, where we had our meals. The house also had lavatories, bath facilities, a lounge for writing, reading, and games. The lectures on dog training were given here. The instructors were professional

German dog trainers who really knew their craft. The trainers were friendly and patient.

Each dog was kept in its own kennel. They were of all types, e.g., Shepherds, Doberman Pinschers, Terriers, mixed breeds, Collies, Cocker Spaniels, Schnauzers, Bloodhounds, Beagles, etc., large and small. We were told that dogs were being trained for guard duty at military storage and supplies depots. These dogs were for the most part voluntarily given to the government at the request of the military.

Each day, we followed a set routine. Morning reveille at 0700 by recording bugle. Dressed, then to the main house, washed, whatever, etc., and on to the main dining hall. A buffet breakfast was set up of scrambled eggs (made from dry powder), rolls, choice of pork sausages, bacon or ham, mashed potatoes or pan-fried, coffee and cake or sugar buns. Very satisfactory. Then, to the kennels to pick up the dogs. Each of us picked one, using a choke chain. It sounds worse than it is. It is a leather leash at the end of which is a chain like ring which is placed over the dog's head and rests loosely over the neck. The leash is held loosely by the trainer in his right hand, but the dog is kept on the left side as the trainer walked. The chain rests more on the dog's shoulder than on its neck. However, when the leash is pulled in concert with the trainer's command the trainer snaps the leash with his left hand. The chain is tightened around the dog's neck, which impedes his movement. In time, by repetition, the dog catches on, and eventually will respond to commands alone.

Dogs, in a way, are like children. They will respond to praise, "Good dog . . . good dog," and a pat on the head. If I were to train a dog at home, I would slip him a small piece of dog biscuit. As time goes by, most dogs accept with approval the commands and companionship of the trainer, and they seem to look forward each day toward being picked up for training. The use of the choke chain was not injurious in any way.

Basic training consisted of placing the dog along the left side of the trainer to walk in place, no pulling, no diversions, no sniffing other dogs or trees, complete discipline. The basic commands were heel, stop, sit, stay, watch, jump (over obstacles), and listen. The idea was to teach the dog to respond to command instantly just as a soldier is trained to do in basic military training. After all, the dog was also in military training. (*Mr. Dog, You're In the Army Now.*) We moved in formation three lines abreast.

And so the weeks went by. By November, the cold, damp weather set in. I caught my usual head cold to which I seemed to be allergic at that time of the year. I reported to the master sergeant, Hassenpheffer, on sick call, and he referred me to the post medical clinic down the road. After a checkup and two aspirins, I was referred back to the master sergeant for duty. On my way back, I met the master sergeant. I gave him the doctor's report.

"OK," he said, "change to your fatigues, report to the supply sergeant, and ask him for hip boots and a long-handled ax. Then report to Johnny (Sergeant) across the road. He'll be waiting for you."

So, I changed to fatigues, reported to the supply sergeant, and I told him as requested by the master sergeant, and I was given a long-handled single edged ax, and a pair of hip boots, size eleven . . . the best he could do. My shoe size was a nine, but it did not matter, except that as I walked with them, my feet moved hither and yon and sideways inside. The top of the boots checked into my crotch and kept irritating it as I walked out of supply, *klippety-klopping* down the pathway to the edge of this plot of land overlooking the roadway.

When I got there, I looked down the road where I saw Johnny standing, his ax leaning up against a tree. He appeared to me to be the size of Paul Bunyan—tall, broad shouldered, strong arm muscles, large heavy hands—no doubt a man of the soil. The plot of land on which I was standing sloped down about four feet to the road.

Johnny noticed me as I descended the sandy slope, sliding down on my heels. I *klippety-klopped* across the road to his side. "What happens now?" I asked.

"Well," he replied, "just look down the road," as he turned his face to his left.

I looked down the road and saw a small figure moving in our direction. The small figure was two figures. There was a soldier on a horse *klippety-klopping* along the road. I had a peculiar premonition that I was about to experience my first adventure . . . or my first misadventure.

The horseman (cavalry) stopped the horse near us, acknowledged our greetings, and then brought the horse onto the grass alongside us. He rode the horse bare-back. He slid off and detached the reins and bridle bit from the horse's mouth. He then took his revolver out of its holster, placed the point of the gun against the horse's right temple, and BANG!! Johnny and I stepped backward. The horse reared up, its front legs churning in the air in protest. My whole body quivered in harmony with the animal. Its legs came down as its body leaned to the right, and plopped over with a loud thud. Its mouth was foaming and its nostrils were snorting. I was astounded and sickened by this horror. The calvary man put his revolver back in its holster, saluted us and said, "Well, it's all yours now," and sauntered off.

I looked down at the horse. The left eye was open and staring at me accusingly. In some telepathic manner its thoughts penetrated my consciousness. It flowed like that without pause. "Is this the way you treat me, I, who have made your civilization possible, I and my cousins have opened up this country for you, I pulled your plow, drew your carriages, wagons, transportation vehicles, military weapons, cannons, and supply carts, I carried mail and messages. Country doctors depended on me to care for the sick and disabled in country and city, etc., etc., and this is my reward?"

"Let's go, Soldier. We have work to do." Johnny's voice awoke me from my trance. It was really only for a brief moment. "You take the neck next to the horse's head. I will take the neck next to its shoulder," and with that he raised his ax above his head and brought it down with a tremendous chop. The horse's blood spouted upward, and in sympathy, the contents of my stomach also spouted upward from the stomach up along the tube to my mouth. I tasted the bitter bile and acid. I was sure my face was turning green as I felt the blood from head and face drain downward. I was beginning to feel woozy. The sergeant looked over at me.

"What's the matter, Soldier? Are you sick?"

"Yes, Sergeant, I don't feel so good," I murmured.

"OK," he said, "ask the master sergeant to send me another man. Leave your ax here."

It wasn't the sight of blood that made me sick. It was the whole darn procedure; butchering this very fine animal. I had a great affection for horses. I also realized that chopping off the horse's head would not be the end of it. Then there would come the cleaning out of the horse's innards. The thought of doing that alone would probably send me to the hospital.

I staggered across the road and tried to ascend the sandy slope, but I kept slipping and finally, in disgust, I got down on my hands and knees and inched my way upwards until I reached the top on all fours. Right there, as I looked up to get on my feet, was Master Sergeant Hassenpheffer looking down at me with apparent wonderment.

"What's the matter with you, Soldier?" he exclaimed. "You look sick."

"Yes," I assured him, "Johnny would like you to send another man."

"Ay! Ay! Ay! You city guys ain't worth a damn! Get over to the cookhouse and give them a hand."

(*"Not being worth a damn" in time came to me as one of the best de-*

15

scriptive attributes of my outward appearance in the military. It saved me from many a "life expendable" mission. His characterization of my person did not bother me a bit. I did not look to climb up the ladder in this "corporation.")

I trudged over, *klippety-klop,* to the cookhouse, and I reported to the sergeant, also known as Sergeant Pferdfleischman.

"OK," he said, "give those guys a hand." He was pointing to a truck that was delivering sacks of meal at the door of the cookhouse. I joined the guys in spite of the queasy feeling I still had in my stomach. A sack of meal was thrust upon my right shoulder. It staggered me. I wobbled into the cookhouse. A hazy, sweet-smelling, sickening air greeted me. Two gnomes stood on a wooden platform overlooking a very large copper vat that was positioned over a grating through which flames penetrated. One gnome was revolving a large wooden paddle around the inside of the cooking vat, while another gnome alongside him was tossing pieces of horse meat and emptying a sack of meal after each toss.

In time, the mush was considered done, and the cooking gnome was handed empty pails which he filled and handed back to us. We put them on the truck. Four of us hopped on, and off we went to the kennels. There we filled the doggie bowls in front of each kennel with a slab of mixed mash for the dog's meal on their return from their training field.

When this was completed, we hopped on the truck and returned to the cookhouse. We washed the pails and then went back to our tents. Our duty was done. When I got to my tent, I slumped on to my cot, shoes and all, and fell asleep. When I awoke, it was already dark, but not too late that I could not go to the dining hall for dinner. I did feel much better, and I was hungry. I could not look at a meat meal from the pot, but I did have a light meal of vegetables, some chicken, and coffee. I was fortunate in having a good sound stomach in spite of occasional upheavals.

The days at the camp continued as usual. It was November and the weather was getting colder. We were given orientation on caring and grooming of dogs, recognizing symptoms of sickness and such, and need for periodic checkups at the vet's, which would be stationed at warehouses and supply dumps overseas. When our training was completed, we would receive a technical sergeant's rating. We would be in charge of five or six dogs at a vet's station overseas. We were required to train soldiers assigned to guard these installations with dogs as companions.

Basic training completed by the end of November, we were ready for advanced training to be conducted at Fort Robinson Remount Station in

Nebraska. We received travel orders (about twenty of us) to board trains at Richmond, Virginia, and on through Kansas City, change for a train to Lincoln, Nebraska, from there a shuttle to the small town of Chadron. There we were met by trucks and taken to the Fort.

The Fort was a well-established installation. We were lodged in a large brick building, steam-heated, individual barracks with single beds and mattresses, very cozy. No complaints in spite of cold weather. There was also a large open community hall with tables for card playing, desks for writing, benches and chairs, and narrow canvas cots that one could relax on, read, nap, lounge, etc.

As we became acquainted with the grounds, we found the entire fort, in general, was very extensive. There were many buildings, corrals filled with horses, and also, of course, cavalry soldiers.

There were also administration buildings run by friendly female civilians who were native to the area. The land was very expansive, stretching as far out to a distance that met snow-capped hills and mountains (part of the Rocky Mountain chain, I surmised). It was already winter, and the air was dry, cold, and nippy, but exhilarating in a way. One could sense the influence that this country could have on the openness and broad expansiveness of personality that is projected by the natives here.

The first order of business was a march down to the medics for physicals and short-arm inspections (very frequently done). Then, a meeting in the building auditorium where we were met by the commander of the post, a colonel (with the two chickens on his shoulders), who briefed us on the daily agenda, etc., etc., Reveille at 0700, breakfast at 0800, 0900 pick up and training the dogs, three hours. Lunch was at 1200. We resumed training the dogs at 1300 till 1600 (one P.M. to four P.M.), then return the dogs to the kennels. Dinner was at 1800 (six P.M.). Then free time in the community room until lights out 2200 (ten P.M.). Not bad.

At the beginning of the training period, we reviewed the basics with the dogs, already quite trained in that. The advanced training was for us to learn, and then to teach the dogs hand signals. The ultimate lesson was to teach the dogs sentry duty, awareness of an intruder, alerting the sentry by stopping or lying down, and looking to the sentry for instructions. The sentry, alerted, would softly say "Watch, easy." If the intruder is spotted, there would be the command, "Go get him." Training the dog to attack called for a special procedure; most untrained dogs would attack an intruder at the legs. This would put the dog in jeopardy. Instead, the dog had to be taught to jump for the arms or hands, especially the one carrying a gun. The dogs

17

were trained not to be intimidated by gunfire. This procedure was the most difficult of all, and it called for patience and encouragement.

One of the fellows was called upon to volunteer as the intruder (not for me). The volunteer was dressed in wicker straw. No problem there. Farmers were a hardy and handy bunch. The wicker straw was interlaced and spread over a thick padding of cotton as lining, sewn in patches. This was tailored into a suit, from head to toe and arms. The face was especially protected with this material. In his right hand he held a gun with blank bullets. When the dog, guided by the leash, was given the command to attack, the intruder would fire the gun. At the beginning of the training, it was expected that the dog would recoil, and then attack the feet of the intruder. In time, he would be trained to attack the arms. Both the trainers and dogs developed a new pride and confidence that comes with successful performance. This was a daily routine except for a half day on Saturday. We had Sundays off. Also there would be groups arriving for dog training, especially marines.

But as military life would have it, nothing runs smoothly day to day. One day as the training session ended, and we were leaving the field with our dogs, one could never imagine anything as horrendous could be happening as the sight we came upon.

As we passed by, there was a marine beating a screaming terrier that was hanging by a choke chain. He was beating the dog with a section of garden hose! No! he was walloping the screaming dog with a section of garden hose! No! He was slamming the screaming dog with a section of garden hose! No! He was whipping the screaming dog with a section of garden hose! I looked on with dismay—this could go on with the civilian dog trainer looking on with approval?

As I turned to move away, one of our original group, who was standing nearby, walked up to the trainer and said, "I know you. You come from the same town in New Hampshire where I live and in which I am the local reporter of the town newspaper. If this is the way you train dogs here, I intend to write and submit a column describing all this to my newspaper." This called for a lot of *chutzpah*.

The trainer looked at him, surprised, to say the least. "If you know what's good for you, don't do it! I would never do a thing like that, especially in the military." With that, the trainer turned and walked away. The marine was still at it—*E-E-E-E-yahuhuh!*

That evening, in the community room, as I laid on a cot reading a paperback book, there were some of the fellows in a corner having a heated discussion. Nothing new. I had no idea what it was all about. Then there was quiet. One of the fellows approached me with a long pad in his hand and said, "We are submitting a petition to the commander telling him of the practice of training dogs by beating them with apparent consent of the civilian instructor. We feel that this practice is inhumane and contrary to everything we were taught at Fort Royal. We would appreciate it if you would add your signature to this petition." Gladly! I added my signature. I noticed that about fifteen others had already signed the petition. I am generally not inclined to sign petitions. I signed a petition in Washington, D.C. when I was working there. Something of no real significance, I thought. Two weeks later, I was investigated by the FBI. You never know in what manner a signature could be used. Nothing came of it, but I became aware that it was possible for the initial preamble to be detached and a new one added. But this petition was worthy of presentation, come what may. But you see, the "way" did come.

A few days later, a notice was posted on the board calling for all personnel to assemble in the auditorium at 0900. When we assembled as directed, the commander of the post came in—the one with two chickens on his shoulders, with his aide-de-camp, a major, and the civilian dog trainer. They took seats on the podium up front. The colonel came to the dias, put his papers on the desk in front of him, and said with consummate authority, "I have your petition, and I want it well understood that what is in them will stop right here! If this gets out to any local newspaper, I'll ship the lot of you to the South Pacific, without the dogs! Is that understood The dog-training at this institution is under the direct supervision of the civilian trainer, and his methods are not to be questioned! Is that understood? When this session is over, you will all assemble at the training field without dogs. Any questions?" (*What questions We understood! The roof had fallen in!*)

"OK, fall out and in platoon formation, the non-coms will march you all to the training field."

Outside, we formed ourselves as instructed and off we marched to the field. We were subdued. No words were spoken. *The South Pacific, gosh almighty!* When we got there, we were instructed to form a single file in front of the field administrative office. The ordeal was not over yet. The officers and trainer then showed up and entered the field office. *Now what was this all about?*

One by one, we were slowly ushered into the office. As one came out, another went in. When my turn came, in I walked. What transpired was incredulous! I found myself standing before an inquisitional board that Jesus Christ must have gone through before the hearing set by Pontius Pilate. Please forgive the allusion, no comparison, of course. The colonel spoke up. Without an at ease from him, I was stiff as a board.

"We would like to know what your feelings are about the way we discipline dogs here." He did not use the term "beating with a rubber hose."

"Well, I replied, with all due respect, Sir *(for one must always preface one's remarks to give the officer his due)*, we were told back in Fort Royal, Virginia by our trainers that treating dogs harshly loses its effectiveness in the long run. The dogs never get over it, and their behavior can become erratic at times. Besides, most of the dogs we train were house pets, and some from dog pounds freely given by the owners to the U.S. Army as their contribution to the war effort." The more I spoke, the more I knew that I was sinking myself into a terrible void from which there was no return. In essence, my statement was in a way a harshly worded criticism of the way things were run at the training field. *Such chutzpah! The hell with it! I had to get it off my chest, even if it would bury me*—which it did, under a pile of dog shit!

The three judges looked surprised and somewhat taken aback that I had the nerve to tell them off. The Colonel leaned forward and looked me squarely in the eyes and said, with imperious dignity, "Oh! So you are the ringleader!"

"The fellows presented me with this petition, which I just signed. There were about fifteen other signatures on that sheet. I felt inclined to support them inasmuch as I felt as they did."

"Well!" the Colonel exclaimed. "If that's the way you feel, I am taking you out of dog training! You will report to Sergeant Nichols at the kennels tomorrow at 0900 in fatigues." And so I was inscribed in the Book of the Fallen; what was known as the shit list, as a *Hund Dreck Handler* (dog shit handler). I could not help but feel that I was being crucified on a cross of dog shit.

The next morning at 0900, I reported at the kennels where I met Sergeant Nichols, the hundt dreck meister, and two other hundt dreck handlers. One of the handlers was told to mount the truck in the back. The other one and myself were given a scooper-dooper set of a long handled pan and brush with which to scoop up the dog shit as the truck moved along the row of kennels. The two of us scooped up the dog shit into the pans, which we gave to the handler on the truck. He emptied the contents into a large empty metal drum. Next to him was another drum filled with lime. I felt sorry for the guy on the truck because he had to take that odoriferous aroma of dog shit as it rose up from inside the drum, which could be overpowering, to say the least.

As I went along, I thought of the peculiar circumstance I found myself in. I had spent eight years striving to attain a bachelor's degree in Social Science, studying Sociology, Anthropology, Abnormal Psychology, Social Psychology, the physical sciences, English literature, history of western civilization and art, French and Spanish languages, and a few other subjects. And here I was, scooping up dog shit. (*This is the Army, Mr. Jones.*)

Finally, after getting through the kennels, we hopped on the truck. The sergeant drove the truck to the refuse field. There, the truck was backed up to the edge of a very deep pit. The drum was turned on its side in the truck, and we proceeded to empty it with long-handled shovels. This was a stinky job if there ever was one. After that was finished, the sergeant scooped up shovels of lime and tossed that over the dog shit in the pit until completely covered. Then we took ourselves off to the post vehicle compound, where we washed the smell thoroughly out of the drum. Then, to the barracks we went, straight away. When I got there, I was ready for a soapy shower and change of clothing. On the way to my cot and locker, I checked the notices on the board. Much to my relief, I found my name listed for barracks orderly the next day. I notified the Master Sergeant that I was coming off duty at the kennel.

The next day I reported to the barracks all by myself after the men left for the training field. This job was clean and easy, just check if the cots were made up, wipe the window sills, open the windows for airing, and sweep the floor. Nothing much else to do. The Master Sergeant would turn up, look around, say a few words, and leave. All this was done in the morning. In the afternoon, I spent my time reading or writing home to wife and family. I cannot recall how many days I was listed for this duty. However, the next day, my fate was decided. I noticed on the board that an opening for stock clerk was offered in the supply room. Without hesitation, I hurried to the Administrative Office, and told the master sergeant that I wished to apply for the clerk position for which I felt qualified by my MOS rating (admin-clerical). He checked my chart and approved my request.

"OK, report to Sergeant McCullen in the supply room tomorrow at 0900." *Hallelujah!*

The next morning, I reported to the supply room—the basement—where I met Sergeant McCullen, a lanky fellow who welcomed me with a ready, pleasant smile; somehow from the side of his mouth, and in a very knowing way. I was also introduced to his dog, a mutt (mixed breed), lying quietly near the sergeant's desk, named Sam. I found it to be well trained and a performer to boot on stage as well as off, very intelligent and pleasant as his master. The dog was good company.

We all got along very well, and I soon settled in very comfortably. The sergeant was from Oklahoma, and spent his leisure time, which was a lot, composing Western songs which he sang accompanied by his guitar. Very pleasant indeed! I also met the supply officer, Lieutenant Maxwell (for want of a better name), who appeared about once a week to check on our operations, and to take care of any problems we might have. I got along with him very well. He was an instructor of American History at a New England college before entering service, very friendly with no prejudicial hang-ups. He asked me about my educational background, which led to many discussions on contemporary events as well as on the significance of past historical events. In time, I was given a Corporal rating (as called for by the T/O), which raised my pay an additional $10 per month, and entitled me to separate quarters in a single-framed house on the post, that had accommodations of two units, more like studio apartments. I settled in very comfortably. I had neighbors there, a regular army non-com and his wife (both middle-aged), both very pleasant and friendly. We got along very well. Things were looking up.

This was about December 1942. Nebraska being a northern state below the Dakotas was subject to the cold weather that blasted its way down from Canada. Sometimes it hit as much as fifteen degrees below zero during the daytime. If the sun came out, the temperature could arise above freezing. Dog-training continued. We maintained and issued the necessary winter clothing—heavy coats, jackets, sweater, socks, underwear, boots, caps, etc. One other duty I had as corporal, was to welcome new groups of soldiers from various military outfits, including Marines, who were sent to take up dog training. My duty, besides issuing them their supplies, was to set them three abreast in military formation, and march them to the medics for physical examination, and then back to the barracks. Nothing to that.

There were three other Jewish fellows in training, and every Friday evening, we assembled in the chapel on the post where a Protestant chaplain greeted us for religious services. They consisted more like discussions of various chapters in the Old Testament. We found them very interesting, and we welcomed this display of consideration of our religious upbringing.

22

The four of us would get together for socializing, and to take trips around the surrounding area on Sundays, time off. One trip we took; hitchhiking, was visiting the Sioux Indian Reservation on the border of South Dakota, which we found very informative and interesting. In service from the beginning, I was already taking photographs with my 620 Kodak box camera, which I carried all the way to France with me. On other Sundays, when it was sunny and clear, I would walk down to the corrals, set myself up on a wooden rail, and look out on the landscape ahead. The air was cold and crisp, but comfortable.

Out in the distance, one could see the blue, snow-capped mountains, which I assume were part of the Rocky Mountain chain. In the foreground were horses moving about in their corrals. I became enveloped in the beauty, the openness, and expansiveness of the whole area, and I could appreciate how much it tends to influence the firm character and openness of the people living here.

At the end of December, about the twenty first was our wedding anniversary, a day to be remembered. On an evening that was windy, snowy and about ten degrees below zero, fully dressed in heavy woolen clothing, I stood out on the road leading out of the post, with my right arm and thumb pointing that-a-way, asking for a lift to town. It did not take long before an army sedan car stopped, a door opened and I heard a most welcome voice, "Come on in!" I hopped in and I landed in the middle of two young lieutenants in the back seat. They opened the conversation with me concerning my background, where I came from, what outfit I was in, so forth and so forth, very pleasant, nice guys. They asked "what the hell" was I doing on such a miserable freezing night. So I told them, and they nodded. It was a warm, pleasant ride. We arrived in the small town of Chadron. I got out of the car, thanked the lieutenants, and looked around. I noticed a portrait photographic studio, which was open. I walked in and found myself in front of a very attractive young woman who introduced herself as the photographer. She led me to the chair, posed me, took three shots. In no time, I found myself presented with three terrific studio portraits. I could not believe how well done they were, here in this small town, somewhere in the corner of Nebraska. Then I was off to a souvenir shop where I bought two medium-sized glass balls filled with water and artificial snow flakes. Each had a small horse drawn wagon and figure, that you turn upside down, and set it down so that figures are enveloped in falling "snow." *Kind of corny, isn't it?* I had all the items including photographs, packed for mailing and sent off to my wife. I got back to the post the same way—by hitching a ride on an army supply truck.

In late January of 1943, the Supply Lieutenant sent me off on a two-week furlough to New York City. I got my travel vouchers, and was driven to the rail station in Chadron, where I took the train to Lincoln. There, I called my wife and gave her the details of the train schedule, and to meet me in Penn Station. I then boarded the train for a direct run through Chicago to New York City; a day and a half traveling. When I arrived at Penn Station, I was met by my wife, and then off to Brooklyn by cab. We spent enjoyable days together, and I also had the opportunity of seeing my mother and father. Time came to return to the post, traveling the same route back.

Sometime in March 1943, I was notified by the administrative office to appear at a certain building to take tests for the Army Specialist Training Program (ASTP). I and two other fellows took the tests which were somewhat similar to the IQ and aptitude tests I took at Camp Lee when I entered service. It took about two and a half hours, and was proctored. When it was over, I turned in my papers, and summarily forgot all about them. I did not realize then how much they were going to change my world. Time moved on in the usual manner. The weather improved and I felt very comfortable. But that was to take a nasty turn.

One day I marched a newly arrived contingent of Marines with close-cropped skulls, straight and firm of stature, ruddy faced, more Germanic than American. I had great respect for them because they took the worst beating in the South Pacific. They came also for dog training. I marched them to the medics and brought them back. I led them to the basement supply, and I issued the usual clothing, bedding, and other necessities for their comfort. I notified them to submit their laundry in a special cloth sack, which I provided, with a blank tag for name and outfit. This was to be submitted once a week. Well! Who could anticipate the worst that could possibly happen? In time, one marine brought his laundry down to the supply room, untagged, and slapped them on the counter in front of me. The drawers were caked with dried fecal matter—shit, in the vernacular. I took one look at them, then looked up at the marine, and pulled out an empty laundry sack, looked up at the marine, told him to bag his laundry, tie the bag, write his name and outfit on the tag, and then bring it down to the supply room. The marine grabbed the items, made some noises under his breath, and stalked out.

A couple of hours later, when I was alone, the marine stalked in, and as was his custom, threw the laundry sack on the counter, leaned over to catch my ear, and declared in a whisper, "You fuckin' Jew bastard. If we ever get you in town, we'll beat the shit out of you!" There it goes again, "shit!" His declaration did not bother me as to the beating. It was the anger and anti-Semitic sentiment that disturbed me (like a Nazi thug). I said nothing, although I felt like shoving my fist down his throat. It would have availed me nothing, knowing that I would never be supported by the colonel. I kept quiet, turned my back on him, and walked to the rear of the room.

The marine left, and when Sergeant McCullen came in, I said nothing about the incident. Neither did I mention it to the Lieutenant. Looking for a sympathetic ear, I went upstairs to speak to Corporal Gold, the mail clerk. He was Jewish, but I had little to do with him. He was man in his thirties who had volunteered to do his "part."

However, this was not the end of the story. About a week later, the major (assistant to the colonel) visited the supply room with supply officer, ostensibly for inspection. The aforementioned marine stayed outside the counter, and pointed me out to the two officers. The major checked the shelves, spoke to the sergeant about the operations of the supply room (evidently checking up on me), etc. and etc.

The major spied a typewriter on one of the counter shelves and asked the sergeant, "What was it doing there?"

The sergeant replied it was in use, and that he (pointing at me) was practicing his typing on it.

The major looked at the sergeant and with an imperious tone of voice declared, "Get rid of it. He won't be needing this!"

That was it! I evidently was on the proverbial shit list again! I had visions of being shipped over to the South Pacific, *again!*

The two officers conversed for a moment, and then walked out, followed by the marine. I looked over to the sergeant, shrugged my shoulders, and told him the whole story. I was resigned to the inevitable, whatever that may be. The sergeant was more sympathetic, and tried to reassure me.

However, fate stepped in, as it was to do so many times thereafter. A few days later, I was called up to the administrative office, wherein was enthroned the colonel, with the two chickens on his shoulders. I was sure that that was *it*. I approached with racing heartbeat. But it was not *it*. Instead, it was something quite unexpected. The Great White Father, bless his soul, in Washington, D.C., turned out to be my savior.

The colonel notified me that I was accepted into the ASTP (Army

Specialist Training Program) and that I was to leave the next day by train, destination: the Star Center at the University of Wyoming, Cheyenne, for briefing. *Hurrah! Back to Academia!* My orders and transportation vouchers were already prepared, and I was to receive them the next morning when transportation would be provided to Chadron. From there to Lincoln by train, and then another train to Cheyenne. I could hardly contain my joy at the thought of leaving this rotten place. However, there were a few people with whom I got along very well, for which I thanked them when I notified them that I was leaving. They saw me off. The only real benefit I got out of my stay there was my corporal ranking. This rating at another time and place almost did me in.

When I arrived at the Cheyenne train station, there were other soldiers who got off with me. We were led to a military troop carrier bus which took us to the university. Through the bus window, as the bus ascended, I was captivated by the sight of the blue, snow-capped hills that stretched up sharply, reflecting the warm-colored light of the sun. The air was clear, dry, and brisk. There is nothing like nature to lift one's spirits.

When we arrived at the university, we were assigned to our quarters, had lunch, and we were notified to appear in the auditorium at 1330 (1:30 P.M.). We assembled there at that time and were seated. A colonel appeared on the platform, and to our surprise gave us the best news yet.

"You fellows are chosen for this program because you all are an elite group of men. After testing, each one of you will be assigned to one of several programs of military government and administrative functions that are necessary for the smooth performance of military operations. The period of training and studies will be nine months, whereupon satisfactory completion by each one of you, the rank of administrative, supply, or lieutenant officer will be granted.

Well, well, things were really beginning to look up. Recognition at last!

"The programs will include military government operations, and studies in the language, history, geography, culture, etc., of a particular country over which the military would have full authority. You will act as an aide to the administrative officers in charge, as interpreters and as advisors on local customs, industry, daily living habits, and matters of importance to the inhabitants. The other programs are administrative in nature, viz: personnel, office practice, graves registration and military cemeteries, supply, procurement, etc., etc. You will participate in a series of tests so

26

that we may determine the best programs in which to place you. The time and place for the tests will be posted outside this room."

Two days later, the time and place for these tests were posted. The next day, about one hundred of us were seated in the auditorium. The tests were handed out, and I found myself faced with sheets of questions separated into sections that included language (French and Spanish that I had previously indicated that I had studied in high school and college), general questions on approaches to personnel, administrative, clerical, organization procedures, reading and interpretation of manual instructions, as well as comprehension and exposition of written instructions of all types.

I was hoping to get into one of the administrative programs, and I did my best not to do too well in the languages. But it did not do much good. A few days later, I found my named posted in the Spanish language and culture area for military government. Why the government thought it necessary to train personnel in the Spanish area was beyond me. It is possible that there was some thought that Spain would get involved? Whatever, it was just as well for me.

The wonder of it all was a notice posted with the names, including mine, of about twenty of us, to pack our duffel bags and to assemble the next morning in the court area at 0900 to be taken to the railroad station in Cheyenne, for a railroad trip to (of all places) Princeton University, New Jersey. *Hallelujah!* I called my wife to tell her the good news, and that I would contact her when I arrived in Princeton.

It took a day and a half traveling by railroad, and we got to know each other in short time. I felt I was among my peers, for a change, people who were university trained and educated. Conversation ran smoothly, experiences swapped, jokes and laughter abounded. By the time we got to Princeton, we had established a friendly rapport with each other. For the next nine months, we were going to have a terrific time together. We had a mixed group of religious affiliations, of which eight were Jewish, the remainder were split evenly between Protestants and Catholics. There were no hang ups regarding this. It was the least important of any of our considerations.

When we arrived in Princeton, we were taken to the University, where we were quartered. The next morning, we were assembled in the auditorium and we were informed of class schedules, meal times, liberty for study, sports, and leave passes to spend weekends in New York City. The weekends to New York City were the best part of my stay at Princeton, which allowed me to arrange meeting my wife at Penn Station. It could not be better. So, all in all for nine months, five days a week of schooling, and two days of real pleasure.

The courses at Princeton were quite extensive and intensive. In the Spanish area, we had the grammar, reading, and writing given by a University instructor. Also, Spanish history and culture, conversation periods with three former refugee teachers from the Spanish Civil War, geography of Spain, regional differences, and socio-economic structure. The head of the Spanish Department was Professor Castro, an elderly, stuffy man who lectured on Spanish history and culture.

We were also given a long range of European history and culture by university professors and instructors. The courses included art and art history, demographics, population growth and its effect on social, economic, socio-psychological behavior of people, its influence on wars, cultural conflicts, environment, pollution, plagues, disease, etc. This course, to me, was more sociological to my way of thinking, and was to influence my whole approach to the social problems of peoples and nations (shades of Malthus). Besides all this, we were put through one of the most grueling programs of physical training that I have ever been subjected to. It was this program, which lasted throughout the nine month period, which conditioned me to the harsh rigors of infantry training and of combat. I did not know at that time the part it would play in my survival.

It all went very well during the stay at the University, which lasted from July 12, 1943 to April 1, 1944, except for one hullabaloo of an incident incited by some anti-Jewish remarks made by Professor Castro during his lecture on Spanish history on the Inquisition and expulsion of the Jews in 1492. This very learned professor insinuated that the Jews were perfidious in their behavior and collaborators in the Moslem rule of Spain. A couple of the Jewish students in class stood up and laced it into him in Spanish. The rest of us joined them. The uproar was loud enough to be heard throughout the building. We all picked up our books and walked out, much to the astonishment of the professor and of the Princeton grammar instructor who was seated over to the side.

That late afternoon about 4:30, during our usual happy hour, we began a discussion among ourselves on submitting a complaint concerning the professor's attitude toward Jews to the director of the University. However, his wife appeared and pleaded with us not to jeopardize his position at the University since he was a refugee. She tried to convince us that he never meant it as it appeared, and that he was truly sorry. We all felt sorry for her, and decided to overlook this incident. We assured her that we would leave things well enough alone for this time.

It always seemed to me incongruous that this very esteemed professor, a refugee republican from fascist Spain, well-cognizant of the racial theories of European fascists, should hold forth with such ignorant, defamatory declamations. It is well-documented that Jews arrived with the Romans long before the illiterate, ignorant, barbarous Visigoths invaded Spain around the sixth century. The Jews had already brought learning, civilization, economic development, professions, teachers in various Middle Eastern languages, so much so that they were highly prized by the kings and princes during the medieval European period, something that the Christian church could not do, nor wanted to do.

I went to the Princeton library looking for Professor Castro's writings on Spanish history and culture, and I found his book. As expected, I found several pages loaded with this anti-Jewish tripe. My father always had the highest regard for learned professors, philosophers, writers, academics, and imbued me with the same reverence. At times, as I attended college, I thought I should try to apply for a fellowship in the Sociology Department. Some other politician got that appointment. I never regretted it on two accounts: 1. I came to believe in time that learning should be tempered by experience, and 2. that academics were not the "learned, enlightened sages" that I was naively taught to respect (not all of them, anyway). I found, in time, that too many of them were enveloped in all the common frailties of ordinary people, sometimes treacherous and deadly.

There were also other activities that we enjoyed participating in. On warm days, as part of our physical training, we played soccer out on the athletic field. Also, we visited the Spanish Museum in East Harlem, in New York City. It was quite a revelation. We had a group photo taken outside the museum.

I should mention that about the last two months of our stay, a young Latin American instructor from Costa Rica took over our conversation class to give some knowledge of the cultures of Latin America and differences in pronunciation and idiomatic expressions, as well as the history and geography of the various countries. The only lasting impression that was made on us was that the women of Costa Rico were the most beautiful of all in South America.

Little did we know that at the end of the nine-month period, the Ivory Tower existence was coming to a crumbling end. On April 1, 1944, we were assembled in the court area in the evening. A major from Washington, D.C. stood up on a podium and announced that we were going to be assigned to the infantry "To furnish leadership and intelligence to combat units." So ended our fantasy! In a way, we should be thankful for the peace and learning at academia, far from the maddening crowd.

This change of venue transferred us into a soldering trough that introduced me to the real world of fact and truth. I was shoved, as others were, into a vortex that had marked human history throughout the ages—of conflict, bloodshed, annihilation, senseless destruction, megalomania, ignorance, stupidity, far from the heady mists of academia.

We were divided into various groups destined for different military camps and units. I was assigned to a group from Camp Carson, Colorado with the 104th Infantry Combat Division. We were assembled the next day, all packed, and trucked to Richmond, Virginia, where we took the train to Kansas City, and then on another train to Denver, Colorado, and from there on to Colorado Springs for Camp Carson. We arrived late into the night, hungry and exhausted. We were gathered in a large hall where our names were called and assignments to the various company units were given. I, and a few others, were assigned to Company A, 415 Regt., First Battalion. Then off we went, guided by a sergeant, taken to our barracks, shown our bunks for picking, and given other information on the routine of camp procedure. We were a motley bunch of guys, and the instructions went into one ear and out the other. But we managed—eventually.

I became conscious that I was entering a new and unfamiliar universe of discourse. My experience in the States would turn out to be nothing compared to those that laid ahead.

IV

The 104th Infantry Division, 415 Regiment, Co. A, First Platoon

For the most part, the men were southerners, with all the prejudices. They were narrow-minded in their perceptions of the world and the people around them, illiterate, but learned in the practical and sexual arts. For them, the Civil War never ended in defeat. Manual experience was more important than learning. This is still very characteristic of our younger generations. Money, drinking, and sex were the three great passions of successful living. Nothing else mattered much. Hitler and the Nazis had more good points than bad. They were fighting against the scourge of Marxist communism, niggers, and Jews. This became obvious in small bits, surreptitiously, in time.

Most of the training programs took place in the mornings. I was placed in line in one of the squads, First Platoon. In the afternoon, I was assigned to the supply room, where I reported to the supply sergeant. I still held my corporal rating. I felt immediately that I was not exactly welcomed. One thing for sure, the supply job was the most preferred in the infantry unit, especially in combat. I was really surplus, and so I was relegated to a corner at the other end of the room, and told to read the supply manual. The sergeant and his three helpers sat at the diagonal end, socializing and generally schmoozing.

However, the first job they gave me was cleaning a new shipment of M-1 rifles, the bores of which were completely compacted in heavy grease. This meant dipping the bores in a drum of gasoline to dissolve the grease and wiping them clean. On this project, I first met Schraeder, an ASTP man, who was assigned to work with me. He had no supply rating. How he came to be picked for this greasy onerous job, I never learned. Schraeder was of average height, stocky, long torso, short legs. He had a good sense of humor, and he took the army in stride. In time, I was to learn that he was Catholic, but assuredly not a practicing one. He fell out of favor

31

with his family because of this and more so for his criticisms of Catholic Church dogma. But there was one thing he was most attached to, and that was the Gilbert and Sullivan operettas. It almost seemed that he had learned all of their pertinent songs and lyrics by heart. As we proceeded with the chore of cleaning the rifles of grease, he would sound off (Stanza I, *HMS Pinafore*):

When I was a lad I served a term
As office boy to an attorney's firm.
I cleaned the windows and I swept the floor
I polished up the handle of the big front door
I polished up the handle so carefully
That now I am the ruler of the Queen's navee.

These recitals would arise as befitting the frequent mind-boggling, incredulous, incomprehensible, decisions, orders, memorandums, foul-ups, and self-congratulatory display of having completed "successfully" some military maneuver that really ended in a disaster.

I had had some experience with G&S both in English Literature in high school and college, and also at the theater with friends. We took the G&S plays as a comic portrayal of English society at their time. But now with experience and maturity, I could understand the universal quality of them all. I valued his friendship, literate, entertaining, and spirited.

Now back to basics and the barracks. It so happened that we were to share the double-decked bunks. He took the top bunk. As time passed, after a full day's training of one sort or another, we both took off for the USO on the post, and shared the activities and drinks (sodas).

One of the programs we had almost daily was a lecture by our platoon lieutenant, Burns. The lectures were based on our manual on infantry practice. When in combat, I realized that the manual, which each of us received, had hardly been revised since WWI. The lectures pertained to the army practice for the infantry troops in combat. For those practices in combat under fire, the Lieutenant would always end his lectures with a warning and a threat that instead of leading the men, he would follow behind with a pistol in hand, which he would not hesitate to use on any man who would turn his back, and run off the field. This was ridiculous! After a few days with these men, I understood why their morale was as low as I found it.

I found incomprehensible the lieutenant's statement. A common belief was held that an officer would lead his men in combat, not follow behind more or less prodding his men forward under threat of being shot. Was this normally instructed in officer's training? To think that an officer would terminate a lecture in front of men who originated (no less) from the deep south—Appalachia, tobacco road, hillbilly towns, proud, white stock of the Confederacy! Rubbish and nonsense! Any officer who took such action in combat would not last a moment. As it turned out, he came to realize that in combat, and ended up with the nervous breakdown.

When we fell out on our half-hour breaks, one could not help but hear the voices of reciprocal threats of action they would take if and when the opportunity arose. They were all closely attached to each other in small groups of common friendship, home towns, and geographical regions. This common friendship had been built up in eighteen months of maneuvers in the deserts of the west in preparation for fighting in North Africa—which never happened.

The main course of conversation proceeded to one of most interest to them all. Each one did his best to outdo the other in telling of his amorous exploits. Each one gave a detailed description of his adventures of love with girls they met, with housewives and their daughters—invited, it seemed as the man of the house was at work. As each one flipped his tongue in sonorous tones as only a southerner could do, one could only view Don Juan as amateur in his sexual and faulted peccadillos.

As they droned on, it was getting somewhat monotonous. I began to recall my experience, not amorous, but as a voyeur. This was during the 1930s . . . the Depression. I spent a year at City College, class of '35, but had to drop out. My father, as a carpenter, had no work. The housing industry had shut down. There were five sons in the family. I was the middle one. The two older ones found some kind of jobs. The two younger ones were still at school. I was about 18–19, and off I went along Sixth Avenue in Manhattan, with the elevated trains above. The streets along the way were filled with employment agencies offering jobs on 3 x 5 cards pinned to an outside board, for six-to-ten dollars per week as busboys, dishwashers, janitors, messengers, watchmen, and such other low-level jobs. Payment to the agency was the first week's salary.

I was desperate. I could not sit home with my mother staring at me in despair. I managed to land a job as a messenger in a drug store at eight dollars per week; not too bad. I figured I could earn an additional amount in the form of tips, bringing home perhaps a total of fifteen dollars. A good sum, considering that our house rent was twenty-five dollars per month.

The work hours were eight hours a day, six days a week. As it turned out, my expectations were only a dream.

The job was in the upper 50s on Sixth Avenue, near Central Park, a posh neighborhood. This was the first step into the real world, outside of academia. It was in a drugstore at the corner of Fifty-ninth Street, owned by Mr. Ritter, a man of German extraction. When I first met him with the agency's note, I thought I was being introduced to Schopenhauer, the philosopher. His long gray hair frizzled out from the side of his temples. His wrinkled face appeared in a perpetual scowl, with a stare befitting a man who had seen a ghost.

On the top of his head, his disheveled grey hair stood wildly up. He appeared as if he had not slept for a week. This became apparent as I got to know what the conditions were in the store, and why he spent time sleeping in the cellar on a cot he had placed there in order to avoid his creditors.

I sure picked the right place to work in. This guy was slowly going broke.

The income from the store came mainly from the soda fountain patronage. There was practically no stock on the shelves behind the drug counters. As it turned out, my job was not only as messenger, but also as sprinter. My qualifications were well-established. I was a member of the relay team each year in Junior High School, when we honored Athletic Day at the General Wingate Athletic Stadium in Flatbush, Brooklyn. I also participated in other athletic sports in physical training.

So, each day, when a customer would come into the store, and asked for a specific item that was not on the shelves, Mr. Ritter would give me some money on the side. He would say, "Go down the cellar and bring up the item." Then I would open the cellar trap door, jump down the steps two at a time, go out the back door into a yard, go up some stairs which led to the street. Down the street, I would sprint a 50-yard dash to the Rexall Drug Store on Fifty-Seventh Street and Sixth Avenue, and with a huff and a puff would ask for the item, and I would pay for it. I exited the store and ran up to Fifth-Ninth Street, down the stairs to the yard, through the cellar door, up the stairs to the counter where I would produce the item, which was usually a small tin of aspirin. All this was done in record time of eight to ten minutes. This experience proved helpful to me when I had eighty-eights on my tail in combat. Of course, this state of affairs could not go on for long.

About three weeks after I started working there, I reported to work on time only to find the doors of the store locked and bolted. Attached to the window was a notice of bankruptcy issued by the New York City Office of Taxation, etc., and also notifying anyone with a claim against the store to write to that office. Mr. Ritter owed me at least a week's pay. I filed my claim. Much to my surprise, I received a check for eight dollars a month later.

Finding myself without a job, I decided to walk down Sixth Avenue to the corner pharmacy, The Windsor, on Fifty-Eighth Street. Mr. Schultz was the proprietor. I entered the store and asked for Mr. Schultz. I told him of my circumstances and employment with Mr. Ritter as a messenger and drug counter clerk. I asked if there was an opening. He said there was, not only as a messenger, but one who would relieve the cashier and generally help around the store. The hours were from twelve noon to nine at night, each day except Sundays. The salary was ten dollars per week. Figure that one out. I was glad to have it, considering it was a well-stocked store, properly run, a busy lunch counter with plenty of take-out orders in a posh neighborhood. I expected to do well with tips.

There were several people working in the store. There was Sol, who was a little older than I. He handled the cash register behind the cigarette and candy counter. His hours were from 8 A.M. to 6 P.M. He was a nice, friendly person with a slight moustache, heavy set, medium height, very much a "man of the world." In time, I found out that he would "wheel and deal" like any of those who worked in the store, and of those friends who visited Mr. Schultz periodically. Though this period was the early 1930s when the country was economically and financially depressed, there were plenty of sharp, enterprising persons capable of turning over a quick buck. Mr. Schultz was well acquainted with quite a few of them who dropped in for a chat now and then.

Mr. Schultz managed the store with a firm hand. He was respected by his creditors and in good stead. He rarely smiled, perhaps because his years of experience with people taught him to gauge them with a certain cautious skepticism. He was middle-aged and had been around. He was generally reticent, and rather aloof, but on occasion would show a rare gesture of caring. I kept clear of him. He was not married, but had a well-kept woman in his apartment upstairs in the building. I never did meet her. Kept women or even men were quite customary in the neighborhood.

Then there was the registered pharmacist, Percival. Of course, that was not his real name, but he reminded me of one. Anyone coming into the store and approaching him, as he stood behind the counter, would be impressed with his meticulous grooming. He had dark hair and sported a dark moustache. Also, there was that manner of smiling through those partly separated two front teeth, or better still, leering at the tall, gorgeously dressed blondes that approached the counter. He was rather short. His striped suit was always well-tailored, broad shoulders, with well-pressed trousers that tapered down to the ankles. I did not particularly like him, as you can see, but I managed to get along with him as well as could be.

Then there was Jack, the cook, and the manager of the lunch counter. He was a jolly kind of a guy with a deep southern accent. He ran the counter with authority. He was a friendly conversationalist. His most famous customer was Fred Allen, of radio fame. Mr. Allen appeared every morning for brunch, and with his dry humor and newspaper in hand, perused for a tete-a-tete with Jack on the news of the day. From this, he gathered his comments for his radio program.

It must be mentioned that Mr. Allen carried on a sly, comic altercation with Jack Benny, who had his own radio program at the same hour on another station. These effusions of comic wit that vibrated through the air-waves weekly between these two masters played an important part in keeping both radio programs up front in maintaining public interest. Mr. Allen had an apartment upstairs with his wife, Portia. I never met her. I met Jack Benny and his wife, Mary Livingstone, several times in the elevator of his apartment hotel up the street. Neither one ever ordered anything from the store for delivery.

Then there was Bob, the short order cook behind the counter. He was a southerner, but somewhat of a wimp. He had a love for drinking, and Jack tended to be impatient with him.

So much for the staff. I found my contacts with the residents of the apartment hotels along Sixth Avenue, and off to the east and west, much more interesting.

As I delivered my packages on calls from residents, I slowly became aware that the practices of the angels of amorous joys were just as prevalent there as in the red light districts of Europe, but with decorum—there were no red light displays. Appointments were more discreetly made. Contacts, mostly by reference and call, were made with delicacy and with a touch of class. I had no hang-ups of moral religiosity concerning their style of living. On the contrary, when I served the astonishingly beautiful ladies behind the cigarette counter, I was enveloped in such emanation of fragrant perfumes that somehow befogged my senses and set my head whirling and my legs on the verge of buckling. They were usually blondes, some brunettes—tall, very attractive, long-legged (my preference), as fashionably dressed as only a model could be. They were mostly stage entertainers downsized due to theater shutdowns. Since there were plenty of well-heeled out-of-towners, businessmen, and tourists looking for a little on the side, as well as lonely men looking for amorous companionship, etc., these beautiful creatures always seemed to fit the bill. All the more power to them. I could not afford it, but I could enjoy it in fantasy.

And so the episodes began. Across the street, northeast corner, I was repeatedly called to deliver items like cigarettes, candy, over the counter drugs, perfume, and such other unmentionables, to Polly Adler's "A House is not a Home" on one of the floors of the apartment building. I was told to use the freight elevator, which took me straight up to the kitchen where it stopped, and the door opened. I was greeted by the Negro cook who would take the package, which had the name labeled on it. I would wait and the cook would return with the payment and tip—highly gratifying.

The cooking and baking smelled good, but I was never offered as much as a cookie. But there were other compensations. At times, I would see a perfectly formed nude flitting past the kitchen door in the hallway with an "Oh my," cry as she spied me in the kitchen.

On another occasion, I was called to deliver a package to Polly Adler's. When I got to the kitchen floor, the cook told me to go in to see Miss So and So in a particular room, which I did. I knocked on the door. "Come in."

I opened the door and saw an attractive young lady, dressed in a fine robe, propped up on a bed. A well-dressed young man was seated next to her. They were both smiling. He looked at the package, noticed the bill, took out his wallet, and paid it plus a fine tip. Who could ask for anything more? I thanked him, and bid them both a "good-day" and left.

I was beginning to get the hang of it all. The good ladies would call when a John was visiting them who paid freely—as well as tips. This was common practice. I was called to deliver a vaginal douche bulb—I was very innocent then, but I learned, to a woman in the Buckingham Palace Hotel on the corner on West Fifth-Seventh Street. As I surmised, I found a John there, who paid the charge plus.

I was often called to deliver a package to a beautiful, lush, platinum blonde on the corner of Fifty-Ninth Street. She was always propped up in bed, fully dressed in a silk negligée which displayed a bulbous cleavage. In a sweet, mellifluous voice, she asked me for the charge, which she paid readily, plus a fine tip. I thanked her and left with an upsurge of ecstatic headiness. I found out later that she was the mistress of Coty, the perfumer who dropped in occasionally from Paris to shoot the breeze with Mr. Schultz and others in the back room of the store. Coty appeared to me dressed as a young fop, very short, hat slanted in a European, continental style alongside of his right temple, a well tailored suit, almost boyish, with a cane deftly hanging from his right arm, with a ready smile and a pleasant personality.

I was also called to deliver a flat tin of cigarettes to an apartment house on Fifty-Eighth Street and Seventh Avenue. When I got to the apartment, I heard a raft of voices, hilarity, and clinking of glasses coming through the closed door. I pressed the doorbell and a soft voice answered, "Who's there?"

"Boy from the drug store, Ma'am."

The door was opened just enough for the lady of the house to put her arm through. I gave her the package with the bill.

"Just a moment," she replied.

She walked away and I noticed a group of young, pretty women sitting on the laps of others, hugging, kissing, foundling each other. I stumbled into a nest of lesbians! Holy Moses! Before I could digest it all, the lady of the house, fingering a 10" cigarette holder with a cigarette smoking, gave me the money, and noticing my leering glances at the display in the room, promptly slammed the door. Bang! No tip, darn it! But I reconciled myself the thought of having experienced the real world. Naive nonsense.

One afternoon, I was called to deliver a flask bottle of bourbon to the hotel across the street. It was still Prohibition, but it was allowed for drug stores to sell whiskey as medicinal potion. To justify this sale, a doctor's prescription had to be furnished. There was no problem. Mr. Schultz procured a pad of ready-made prescriptions from a local doctor who had his office up the street, a quid-pro-quo arrangement of which I had no knowledge. Mr. Schultz personally wrapped the flask in the back of the store. Then he gave me the particulars—address and the amount of the bill. He then ripped off a prescription from the pad and put it into the drawer after writing the patient's name and address on it. When the supply of whiskey was exhausted, he would make a special call and a few days later, a new case would be delivered. No questions asked. The "used" prescriptions were turned in.

I crossed the street, entered the apartment hotel building, took the elevator to the designated floor, and approached the apartment. Again, strange voices were issuing forth through the front door. Ooh! Ahh! Ahh! It's wonderful! You're terrific! (A female voice.) Ahh! More! More! Again! Again! Oh God! The best I have ever had! Huff and puff, Puff and puff—the male was doing his push-ups. I refrained from pressing the bell button. The sounds receded slowly, and with ecstatic relief after such amorous expression of joy, the climax, and then silence. I rang the doorbell. A male voice wanted to know who it was. I gave my usual reply. The door opened slightly. A man stood there in his undershorts and a nose appeared looking out, the tip of which revealed a one-inch round specimen of the reddest radish you could find—lit up like Rudolph's. I gave him the bottle.

"How much?"

"Twenty-five dollars," I replied.

"Just a moment!"

As he moved away from the door, I noticed a sheet-covered shapely body with a beautiful set of blue eyes, blonde wavy hair, angelic, looking out. How beautiful! How wonderful! What paradisiacal pleasure! I'm sure it beat the pleasures of Adam and Eve. What a life! To be so endowed with such wealth as to enjoy the pleasures of the good life in the midst of the worst of the poverty stricken Depression, demonstrates the capacity of men and women in meeting misfortune with hope and undiminished strength. What else was there? The man gave me the money. Bang! The door shut. Darn it! No tip! I returned to the store.

At the lunch counter, Bob the wimp did not show up, gone, never to return. Mr. Schultz called the unemployment agency for a replacement for a short-order cook. Soon after, there appeared a tall, broad-shouldered, good-looking young man, whose voice resonated as only a professional opera baritone could emit. He had jet black wavy hair, a ready smile, a charismatic bearing. A few words with Mr. Schultz, who then introduced him to Jack, and put him to work immediately behind the lunch counter, change of jacket and apron. I do not recall his proper name, but to me he was Don Giovanni.

Don Giovanni did very well. His pleasant personality and good looks attracted many patrons, especially women, mostly single or widowed. His conversations with them were quite amicable and with proper demeanor. For two weeks, there was one attractive middle-aged widow who appeared every morning, noon, and evening at the counter, and seemed to pay particular attention to him. Well, the inevitable outcome. He left to take up residence with this very appealing, affluent dame as a live-in escort, well kept.

All the more power to him. Who could ask for anything more! A new replacement appeared—a rather nondescript person of no bearing.

One evening, about 6 P.M., I was called upon to deliver a small bottle of perfume, Coty's of course, to an apartment upstairs in the hotel. It was already dark outside. I was instructed to receive payment in cash—no credit! I entered the building, took the elevator to the proper floor, walked to the apartment, and pressed the bell button.

"Who's there" It was a soft female voice.

"Boy from the drug store," I replied.

"Come in."

I turned the doorknob and walked in. I could not believe my eyes at what I saw. Seated before a large oval mirror of a vanity desk, was this very gorgeous-looking blonde—Aphrodite, the Greek goddess, if ever I saw her. She was dressed in a pinkish, silk negligée, the front of which was somewhat apart, exposing the slight edges of her well-rounded breasts, separated by a stimulating cleavage that extended quite a length downward.

She caught the glance of my wide-open eyes reflected in the mirror. She immediately covered the exposed area, looked up at me and exclaimed, "What the hell do you think you're looking at, you blankety, blankety son of a bitch!"

My vocabulary for English abusive words increased tenfold. My earlobes were inflating, hot as pitch. There was nothing more to see than this beautiful Aphrodite, whom in my mind, should be taken off her pedestal. Woe is me! What else was left?

I could never imagine such abuse of the English language could be mouthed by such an angelic-looking Madonna. I was completely devastated. My most cherished illusions of female purity, virtue, restraint, and decorum was completely shattered. She was evidently drunk, inebriated, besotted, *borracho* (Spanish for drunk).

"Give me the perfume!" she demanded.

"Sorry, Ma'am. I was instructed to be paid in cash. The charge is thirty dollars."

"What, that (so and so), he has a lot of nerve refusing me credit. I have been his best customer, that (so and so)!"

She continued with her tirade, and I turned toward the door. This was about as much as I could take. I thought she was going to fling her hair brush at me. I made a hasty retreat to the elevator. As the elevator door closed, there was an unbearable silence as it descended. I was glad to get back to the store, a secure haven. I returned the perfume to Mr. Schultz, and told him she did not have the money. That was that!

A half hour later, the blonde entered the store, wearing a long overcoat over her negligee. She asked for Mr. Schultz. When he appeared, she approached him and begged for the perfume. He shook his head. She leaned over to his left ear and whispered something. Mr. Schultz stepped back in horror as if he had been struck with a bolt of lightning, grabbed her right arm, and hastily strode her to the door, opened it, and thrust her into the night air.

I looked out the window in back of me and noticed that she was staggering in complete befuddlement. I ran out from behind the counter, through the doorway, approached her, and tried to grab her arm.

"Don't touch me, you (so and so)" there she went again. It did not faze me. I told her to follow me to the Hotel entrance, which she did. I turned her over to the doorman. That was that. I never saw her again.

There was a queer duck I shall call Sir Humphrey Winklebottom, who sounded off as a true son of Britain. In spite of the fact that we could hardly take him seriously, we tolerated him and played along with his absurd characterization. He was rather short, wore a black-striped suit, tapered at the bottom, which covered gray spats. He wore black patent-leather shoes. I should make mention of his well-groomed thin moustache, which he displayed with apparent sophistication.

He was a likable fellow, who joked with Jack at the lunch counter at noontime while having his lunch. He displayed a forced British accent as thick as a piece of bologna. From time to time, he was allowed to charge his bill, which he promptly paid whenever he received money from his Pater in England, as he claimed. After not showing up for a couple of weeks, Mr. Schultz gave me his unpaid twenty dollar bill, and told me to go to his address for collection. I walked across to Fifth-Eighth Street toward Fifth Avenue in the middle of the block. When I got to his brownstone building, I walked up the stone steps and rang the superintendent's doorbell. A man came to the door.

"Yes?"

"Does Mr. Winklebottom live here?" I asked.

"Who are you?"

"I am from Windsor Pharmacy."

"Oh! That two-bit four-flusher, that con artist! He wormed his way out one night with his luggage owing me a month's rent," he replied. "If you ever catch up with him, I would appreciate it if you let me have his address."

With that, he shut the door. Bang! Fat chance if we would ever let him know!

I walked down the steps with a whistle on my lips, a song in my heart, and a tap in my steps. That con artist put it over on Mr. Schultz and the landlord. All the more power to him. I never saw him again.

There were many things that went on which could fill a volume, but were not pertinent to the story, except one other thing. Sol, the cashier, got himself another job in one of the apartments upstairs in the building. I took over his job as a cashier during the day from 8:30 A.M. to 6 P.M., six days a week. I received a five-dollar increase. I still retained my prestigious job as delivery boy from time to time.

I had no idea what kind of job Sol had. One day, he called to have sandwich and coffee to be delivered to the apartment. When I got there, rang the bell, he came to the door and opened it.

"Hi yah! How's trix?"

"Fine, fine," I replied.

I noticed a large metal drum installed on top of a wooden crate. At the bottom of the drum was a wooden tap spigot.

"What is that?" I asked.

"Why, there's mineral oil in the drum," he replied.

On the floor, there were several empty half-gallon glass pitchers. He took one of them, placed it under the spigot, turned the knob, and out flowed the mineral oil. When it reached the top of the pitcher, he closed the spigot, and then reached over for a large brown bottle labeled *Iodine*. He then reached over for a large syringe headed with a large bulb, which he pressed to draw up some iodine, placed the syringe over the pitcher full of mineral oil, and squeezed a predetermined number of drops into it. He stirred the mineral oil in the pitcher until a desired tint of golden-brown color appeared, resembling a much desired suntan.

When satisfied, he moved over to a table with pitcher in hand, on which was a compartment type of carton filled with a dozen six-ounce empty screw-capped bottles. He removed the caps, and poured in the tinted mineral oil in each bottle until they were all filled up. He then reached over to a packet of dry, gummed labels, and drew one which he swiped over a wet sponge that was in a large bowl which was slightly filled with water. He placed the label carefully over the bottle, pressing lightly the edges. Each bottle was so processed. Each label carried the price of five dollars with a declaration as to the efficacy of its contents to produce the most irresistible glow of sun tan ever. Very good indeed! In time, his rate of production increased remarkably, and so did the money in his pocket.

This may be right for him, but my job was not right for me. My new hours afforded me the opportunity of returning to City College. I registered for two courses in the evening session, one course for one credit and another for two credits. My father began to work under the New Deal work programs as a carpenter. I was getting older, and felt there was no way out for my future except to obtain a college degree.

It all came to a head one winter when Mr. Schultz, on a Saturday morning, told me that on the coming Monday, I was to go down to the storeroom in the cellar and to clean out all the rubbish. I knew what the rubbish was—nothing but dusty old empty cartons, crates, bottles, cans, fry pans, and God knows what else, including whatever else that crawled. Not for me! I did not say anything. I knew right then and there that I had had it up to my neck. As I received my week's pay on Saturday. I thought it a good time to quit. When I got home, I told my father that I was returning to college full time. He wished me luck, but advised me that he could not help me financially. That was alright with me. I figured I could get a summer job at some hotel in the Catskills. As a youngster, I had spent many summers there with my family when my parents rented, with other families, living quarters, cooking and dining hall facilities on a farm owned by a Jewish couple.

Monday, I sent a letter to Mr. Schultz telling him that I quit. That was that! He could take his stinking cellar and clean it out himself!

I registered at City College for a full-time program, and started to attend classes at the beginning of February 1936. I was in the class of 1939. Back to academia! Home Sweet Home. However, my education in the real world was to continue. Thought must be tempered by the real. My education was just beginning in the real world.

V

Closer to Battle

During April, I kept checking the help wanted ads in the newspapers for summer help in the Catskill Mountains. As luck would have, I found one ad for a job as a bellhop in a small hotel in Hurleyville, New York. The telephone number was indicated. I called, and I was granted an interview at some address in the Bronx. When I got there, I met a middle-aged Jewish couple who were European refugees, with son and daughter-in-law who were American. After speaking with them for a short while, I was offered the job. The pay was fifteen dollars a month, room and board, for July and August. They suggested I buy a bellhop's uniform at a second-hand clothing store, specializing in such clothing. I was told to appear at their home address near the end of June, at which time I would be taken to the hotel with others.

When I returned home, I checked the *Yellow Pages* for a vintage clothing store that sold used uniforms of all types. The next day, I went to Manhattan to Broadway in the thirties, walked up one flight, and in no time, negotiated the purchase of a pair of maroon-colored trousers with blue-bordered white stripes along the sides from the waist down to the bottom held up with suspenders. I became the very model of a major bellhop.

At the end of June, with the end of sessions, I packed my one piece of luggage, bid my parents good-bye, and was off to the hotel in the Catskill Mountains. I could never have imagined the experiences that were to befall me.

There was really not too much to the job. Most guests arrived either late Friday or early Saturday mornings. Some would come Sunday mornings. Some guests arrived in their cars or by private limousine. Others came by train or travel bus. In all cases, the chauffeur and I were there to greet and transport the new arrivals and their luggage to the hotel. For the most part, I took the guests to their room in a three-storied building on the side of the main building, and also up the floors of the main building which housed the kitchen and dining hall. I don't know where I got the strength to lug their baggage up three flight of stairs, but I managed well enough as time went by.

The guests were a motley group of people, mostly women, except on weekends when husbands came. There also were middle-aged widows, unattached women, young singles, with friends, and young women with children. Occasionally, some young unmarried males would show up. There were also a few teenage girls who accompanied their mothers and sometimes their grandmothers. These teenagers, it seemed to me, were always at a loss to find something of interest. It did not take long.

The weekly rate was eighteen dollars to twenty-five dollars, depending on accommodations. Three full meals a day, and an evening snack before retiring, and after the entertainment provided on Friday and Saturday nights. There was dancing every evening, as well. One of my jobs was to set up the snacks consisting of the cakes leftover from dinner, and serving tea, milk, or coffee. I did not mind at all because it did pay off in the end.

In time, I settled into a regular routine by making myself useful to the guests for whatever reason. On Sunday afternoons, when the hustle and bustle of people leaving and arriving was over, I would sit on the veranda alongside the main house and relax. One of the guests, a rather short, plump young woman, came over and sat down in a chair next to mine. She was on her honeymoon with her husband who was a baker, but he had just left to go back to work after spending two weeks with her. I had spoken with her several times before, very casually . . . nothing of real interest for me. She told me quite frankly that she wanted to have a child in the worst way, under any circumstances, married or unmarried. She even propositioned her dentist right in his office, but he turned her down. I thought that showed good sense. So, she finally married a baker—a rather short, plain, thin man, hardly one that would attract women to him. Well, we were talking of this and that, when she stopped and looking straight ahead, she said, "Do you want to do it?"

"Do it?" I replied. "What do you mean, *do it?*" I don't know if I was thick or plainly naive.

"You know," she said as she motioned her fist forward. "*Do it!*"

"Oh yes," I finally caught on. Before I could check myself, I said, "Yeah, I'll do it."

Well, I was committed, not exactly in like Flynn just yet. What the hell, she was married, after all. I figured I had nothing to lose. *Oh, merry me!* So, we arranged a rendezvous in the evening after dinner, up the road and over to one side on the grass.

45

Toward the evening, I was beginning to have second thoughts about doing it, especially with her. But I decided to meet her near her building and we walked up the road in the darkness. About a quarter of a mile up, we left the road and found a grassy spot, which was rather damp from the dew. There was a great deal of traffic on the road, which we did not anticipate. It was noisy and distracting. I developed the feeling that the automobile occupants were watching us. This feeling had no basis in fact, probably due to feelings of guilt.

She lay down on the grass, raised her dress up to her waist, and pulled down her panties. I laid down beside her, unzipped my fly, and took out my phallus. As I rolled over on top of her, an unsettling thought came suddenly to mind. *Holy Moses! I did not have a condom!* If she were to have a child, and if she returned the following year, which she did, I would never know if it was mine! This thought was very disquieting. My phallus became limp. Of course, Aphrodite had no idea of this state of mind. Thinking that I needed more inspiration and encouragement, she grabbed my phallus to stimulate it. Well, it did not take long to extend itself once again. The stimulation was so vigorous that my phallus reached its climax post haste and ejected whatever would naturally spill forward—into the grass.

During this feeble attempt to engross her, my breathing had accelerated with rapid intake of air that sounded heavy, with exhilarating delight. In spite of the fact, to my relief, that I did not complete this coition, I nevertheless felt ecstatic. I slumped down on her with my head between her soft breasts, still breathing rapidly.

"My God, my God," I murmured softly.

She stroked my hair softly and whispered, "That's all right. Don't you mind. The next time it will be better."

I said nothing. I doubted if there would be a next time. She had no idea what had gone through my mind. I had no intention of telling her. Even though my efforts were only half fulfilled, I did have this satisfaction of having felt a woman in love's embrace. To my mind, I had the satisfaction of feeling that I was no longer a virgin. *Hallelujah!*

We got up, made ourselves decent, as the saying goes, and walked down to the road. When we arrived back at the building, we sat down on a bench outside the entrance. As we were talking, the boss came out of the building, looked at us with a disapproving glance, and walked off. As one of my jobs was to put out the lights in the building at 11:00 P.M. every night, unbeknownst to the boss, I saw him regularly skulking down the steps out of the building. So the boss was doing it. He was a man in his fifties, who really worked very hard. He did not get much from his wife as she was sickly, and rarely left her room. He depended a lot on his son and daughter-in-law, and the chauffeur who did yeoman's duty as driving guests to the city and picking some of them up to drive them to the hotel. Also, he drove the pick-up truck for shopping errands to town. So, if the boss was doing it, there was good reason.

Then, there was a most peculiar incident of *l'amour* in the afternoon, when I was approached one day by one of the female guests, smiling with a glee of satisfaction. "Oh," I said, "you seem to be very happy about something."

"Yes," she replied unabashedly, "I must tell you since I began menopause . . ." Mind you, she was taking me into her confidence. Don't ask me why. "I have had the best years of my life." She was a woman in her early fifties, I take it, a widow to boot. "I and my sister have been taking the boys of the band on, behind the handball court up against the backboard, one by one." No wonder I had noticed the boys, mostly seniors in high school, or first year college, skirt behind the court, one by one while playing handball. So-o—the boys in the band were doing it.

In the evening, the boss expected all of the help to entertain the female guests at the dance. The female guests were usually a mixed lot, some married with children whose husband would come up on weekends. Some were middle-aged widows. Some were young singles up for whatever. All the help joined in with glee, and much more. The help was quartered in a single hut, off grounds, which was compartmentalized in quarters. The waiters and the busboys had two compartments. The chauffeur, one, with whatever floozie he could pick up. I had one with Larry, the children's waiter. More about him later.

After the dance, I would hear the waiters and busboys coming in at all hours of the night, discussing their *Don Giovanni* escapades in the privacy of their ladies' boudoirs. *L'amour toujours, l'amour.* So, the waiters and the busboys were doing it.

Occasionally, the chauffeur would noisily enter his bunk with his floozie, both laughing and stomping on the creaking floorboard, somewhat, I could surmise, a bit under the weather. I could hear the bedspring squeak as they both got on it. She laughed as she instructed him on how to loosen, or probably strip, her dress off. It did not take him long to strip his pants off, as he laughingly described it. And so to it . . . doing it! The bed spring squeaked and squealed as he began to do his push-ups.

"Oh my God, oh my God," she bellowed forth. Her breathing was rapid and heavy as she issued forth, transfixed into nirvana. Then silence, except her commendatory remarks, "You're good, you're wonderful!" And so, I did manage to fall asleep, with such vicarious fantasies. Some guys have all the luck. Now I knew the chauffeur was doing it.

One morning, Grandma came knocking on our door. She was crying. We opened the door. There she was, holding a pair of soiled purple panties found on the lawn. She murmured through her tears that her fifteen-year-old grandchild had lost her sweet, virginal innocence. My God! What should she do? Her mother would never forgive her! *C'est la vie.* There was no consoling her, as she drifted away. So the fifteen-year-old guest was doing it.

Then, there was the rather handsome middle-aged wife of a bar owner, whose sixteen-year-old daughter was cavorting with the young Gregory Peck-type of riding instructor, son of the owner of the Horsey Riding Academy up the road. Practically every morning I would see both of them on horse, galloping down the road. She was fairly attractive, broad shouldered, more athletic than womanly. I was not attracted to her. Her mother, who being a woman of this world, rather suspected that their relationship had more to do than riding instruction. The mother was fairly convinced that her daughter was actively participating in and enjoying the many ways of learning to *ride.* In other words, let's face it . . . the daughter and he were also doing it. Was he also giving her lessons in bareback riding?

The mother, who seemed to hold me in some esteem, tried to encourage me to take up with her. I was not interested, and besides, how could I possibly compete against such a hunk of a man? Her efforts came to naught. The mother settled the liaison by cutting short their stay, and left post haste.

Now, there is time for me to talk about Larry, my bunkmate. He was a pre-med student of infinite stamina in the pursuit of *l'amour.* He was the children's waiter, and in time, he revealed to me that he had a harem of willing, and somewhat seductive, group of young Aphrodites (mothers) whose demands were insatiable, as he put it. Somewhat exaggerated, I thought, but containing some grain of truth. On weekdays, at least three times a week, he came into the room about one or two o'clock in the morning and flopped on his bed, exhausted and then off to sleep. Of course, his cavorting was his own business, but there came a time when I had to ask him what it was all about. He was getting thinner and thinner. Finally, he opened up. Some of the young mothers found him so attractive that they tried everything possible to seduce him. I thought he embroidered his amorous forays a bit, but I took it all in with a sense of humor.

By the end of the summer, on Labor Day, he could hardly stand up. The chauffeur and I took him to the train station on his own two feet, but only with arms encircled around our shoulders. A busboy carried his luggage, and assured us that he would take care of him all the way to the city. A few days later, the busboy wrote us—we had to stay to help in closing up the hotel—that Larry had signed into a hospital, suffering from total exhaustion. During his stay there, he had to tell them of the exhausting expenditure of energy in the many amorous contortions needed to bring on the exhilarating climax for both the woman and himself. As the result of this confession, the hospital assigned the following doctors to his beside, e.g., a psychologist to test his libido, a cardiologist to test his heart (EKG), a urologist to test his prostate, a hematologist to test his blood (for anemia), and an endocrinologist to study his testosterone glands for possible hyperactivity. When all the tests were completed, it was concluded that what he needed was a complete rest, an infusion of essential vitamins, and plenty of meat, fruits and vegetables—the *sine qua non* for healthy living. It only took two days for his miraculous recovery, which he demonstrated by skipping over the beds of patients to chase the nurses down the corridors. This was too much for the hospital administrators, who summarily dressed him, packed his bag, and ejected him through the exit door to continue his chase down the street.

This is about it, except that I should mention the sounds that greeted my ears as I went through the halls of the hotel bedroom building each night when I would extinguish the hall lights. The hall was filled with squeaks, squawks, and wails as the bed springs were pummeled in amorous delights. I was affected only to the extent that I thought of the possibilities of composing a sonata worthy of a Stravinsky. His music squeaks, squawks, wails, to tom-tom African beat, "Rites of Spring." It would be entitled, "Hope Springs Eternal."

Well, enough is enough! My mind was stretched (and I guess the reader's as well). The truck, which had been proceeding monotonously on a stop and go pace, finally moved over to the side of the road. The sergeant announced a rest stop. We all got out and each proceeded behind bushes or trees to relieve ourselves. When that was done, we all came back and sat alongside of the truck on the grass and ravished a K-ration can of food and a few swigs of water from our canteens. Then dessert, a fruit bar, or a bar of chocolate which was provided. In a half hour, the rest period was over and we ascended the truck. Off we went, hoping that we could make better time to Rheims, France, where we will stop for a night's stay at a USO rest center.

To continue, I returned to City College with enough money to carry me through for a year in spite of the fact that I helped my father pay the rent for January and February when he was out of work. My specialties in my studies were sociology (major), anthropology, psychology, abnormal as well as social study group behavior, philosophy, Spanish, history of western civilization, and art. Also one credit courses, such as geology, astronomy, public speaking, music appreciation, English literature and exposition, and a few other electives. These courses were spread over a two-and-a-half-year period.

The following summer, I contacted the owner of the hotel, who appeared reluctant to offer me the bellhop's job again. I think he had become wary of me. However, he did offer me a busboy's job, which I took. It was something, anyway. As it turned out, I did fairly well in tips.

That summer, life at the hotel proceeded as usual. Doing it was still on the agenda. I kept away from all this as I concluded that this type of activity could lead me astray. I wanted very much to get my degree, and not involve myself in any amorous peccadillos or entanglements. It just was not worth it. I recalled Schopenhauers *The World of Will and Idea.* Larry came back again as the children's waiter, fully fortified with a supply of B-complex and steroid pills.

When the summer was over, I returned to City College. This was September 1938, and completed a degree in social science (BSS) graduating in June, 1939. I then entered service with the Federal Government in Washington, D.C. I had taken several exams for Social Science Analyst, and Junior Professional Assistant paying $2,000 per year. I had taken three exams, and had a general grade of eighty five on all, an eligibility rating. On each return, it was indicated that I would be called when a position was available. I could not wait. I decided to go to Washington, D.C. to visit the personnel office at the Federal Security Agency.

When I finally found that office, I entered and found an officious-bearing young female staring at me. "Yes? What could I do for you?"

I showed her my three exam notices, and asked if there were any openings. She looked at the notices, shook her head and said, "All of you Social Science students from New York City are looking for these jobs which are not now available. I can only offer you a job as messenger."

I gulped, and stared at her for a moment. I knew she was lying through her teeth. There was nothing to be said. I could not think of returning to New York. I took the job, which paid $1,040 a year. In time, I worked my way up to statistical clerk, which paid $1,440 per year. Before I married, I sent about half of my salary to my parents.

I took up residence at a boarding house in the second alphabet as the city was drawn. I met my wife-to-be there, and we were married in December 1941. But that is only an interlude. Six months later, I was drafted into service. Now back to the infantry.

After two weeks in the infantry training, I was called to report to the captain's office. The first sergeant pointed to the captain's door with a snicker of glee, and told me to enter his office. I entered, saluted, and was told to be at ease.

"Corporal Hanish reporting, Sir," I said.

"I am sorry to tell you, Corporal Hanish, that because of T/O limitations, I am required to reduce you to the rank of Private First Class (PFC). I received notice from headquarters to construct my table of organization (T/O) according to army regulations. As of May 1, you will turn in one of your stripes," the captain announced.

I stared at him in disbelief. Back at the Star Center, in Cheyenne, Wyoming, we were all told that we were an elite group, and after nine months of ASTP training, we would be awarded with either a warrant officer's or lieutenant's rating. After nine months at Princeton, we were told we were being allocated to the infantry divisions to raise the literacy and command quality of their unit. Now I find myself being demoted to a lowly PFC. I said nothing. One moment of silence and I was then summarily dismissed. I saluted, about faced, and left. The 1st Sergeant still had that glare of snicker with glee. I then wrote home to my wife that my rank had been reduced to PFC, and was so to be addressed. I guess I was put out, and it must have shown in my letter.

Well, two weeks later, I was called to see the captain. I had no reason to anticipate what was to occur.

As I entered the office of the first sergeant, who sat outside of the captain's office, I saw a livid, overwrought sergeant glaring at me with spears jutting out of his bulging eyes, and from his mouth a massive flow of white froth. It warmed the cockles of my heart.

"What's up?" I inquired calmly. If there was anything not to say, this lackadaisical mode of innocence infuriated him further. I thought he was about to chew the edges off his desk.

The sergeant leaned forward across his desk with trembling hands, which he waved at me, and said, "You Goddamn (so and so), if there is the last thing I do before I die, I am going to get everyone of you." Meaning, of course, the Jews in the outfit. There were eight of us.

To digress for a moment, the company clerk was a fellow named Spiegel, the only literate one capable of holding the job, except for the other Jews. Every morning, for some unexplained reason, as we were all lined up outside of the office for roll call, the office door would be flung open as Spiegel would be doing a fifty-yard dash through the doorway and running like hell alongside of the building, followed by the first sergeant running in his stocking feet, as he threw his shoes at him, cursing and cussing in words that could never be found in Webster's dictionaries.

This humorous display of wrath which occurred every morning at the same time (you could check our watch by this) reminded me of the Charlie Chaplin escapades of the cinema in the silent era. Spiegel, of course, was Jewish. He was a short fellow, very agile, with a good sense of humor. I could only imagine that the first sergeant from "Looziana" would feel at times that he was sitting on a pad of spiked nails in trying to deal with his company clerk. *Hallelujah!*

To continue. "Get inside, the captain wants to see you."

I knocked on the captain's door. "Enter," came the reply.

I opened the door and walked in. The captain was seated behind his desk, and my platoon lieutenant was seated at the side of the desk to the captain's right. I came to attention, and saluted. No at ease was forthcoming. I was stiff as a board. There was an air of impending doom, like being led to the guillotine.

The captain was holding some papers in his hand, looking at them. He looked up and burst forth, "Where in the *hell* did you get the *nerve* to *write* to Senator Lehman about the loss of your corporal's rating?"

I was flabbergasted. For the captain to think that I would be foolish enough to write to my senator on any matter pertaining to military decisions was beyond me. I suspected that my wife did. She was always overprotective of my mistreated soul. She was inclined to be impetuous at times, characteristic of wives who feel that their husbands do not stand up to the slings and arrows of outrageous fortune, like stout-hearted me.

I stared at the captain for a moment. I could not believe my ears. "Sir," I answered, "with all due respect . . ." You must always preface this remark in any reply of denial to an unfounded accusation, "I did not write to

Senator Lehman. I would never consider such a thing. I don't know of anyone who would do anything like this."

"Well," the captain replied, "I don't believe you. I want you to hear my reply to the senator. 'PFC Alvin Hanish's corporal rating was remitted for the following reasons: he was found to be deficient in leadership. He was incapable of performing the basic elements of infantry training. He was inept at fulfilling the basic duties of a supply clerk as reported by the supply sergeant. He was deficient in following the simple rules and regulations of barrack's orderliness. He demonstrated an inadequate response in following orders and commands on maneuver training. In short, he demonstrated that as a soldier in infantry training, he did not qualify to hold the rating of corporal.' "

Of course, this was overkill. This was ridiculous. I could hardly believe that the senator would possibly believe this tripe. I could only imagine that the captain's reply would proceed up the line through the Regiment Battalion; Corps, General Bradley's office, to the Pentagon, which would undoubtedly couch it in more diplomatic verbiage.

This was not all. The captain was not through with me yet. He leaned over on his bent right elbow on the desk, pointing his right index finger at me, and said, "When we go overseas, in combat, you are going out in front as we walk along the road as point man!" Point man is out in front of the company about twenty feet, supposedly on lookout, but more as a walking decoy. I would have the dubious honor of getting the first shot up my ass. Of course, I would die a hero's death. My wife would be notified of my courageous action in leading the company into combat, for which I would be awarded the Purple Heart and the Bronze Medal for action beyond the call of duty.

"There is nothing else! Dismissed!"

I saluted and as I was ready to maneuver an about face, the Lieutenant issued forth a sagacious, and as profound a judgment befitting only a Solomon, the sage, "It is good to have a relative as a U.S. Senator."

This astounded me. We all know that all Jews are related!? I said nothing as if to acknowledge the truth of his statement. If that is what he wants to believe, who am I to deny it? Besides, it was to my advantage for both of them to think so.

I turned, walked to the door, opened it, and came out to find the first sergeant still frothing at the mouth, with a look that would freeze a tiger in its tracks. I walked out into the open with nary a stare at him, and as I stepped out, with undaunted courage, I muttered to myself, *To hell with you too, you bastard!* From then on, I baptized him Sergeant Momzeur. I recovered my composure. I did not know whether to burst out laughing or to cry. To laugh because this whole scene was ludicrous, or to cry because I felt that God must help us with such ridiculous leaders of a combat infantry company.

When I returned to the barracks, I found Schraeder there sitting by his bunk. I told him what happened. We both joined in a good stretch of laughter, and Schraeder broke out with an appropriate G&S rhyme, *The Mikado*:

A more humane Mikado
Never did in Japan exist,
To nobody second, I am certainly reckoned
A true philanthropist.
It is my very human endeavor
To make to some extent,
Each evil liver
A running river of harmless merriment.
My object all sublime
I shall achieve in time
To let the punishment fit the crime,
And make each prisoner pent unwillingly represent
A source of innocent merriment.

And then II G&S (*HMS Pinafore*):

As office boy I made such a mark
That they gave me the post of a junior clark.
I served the writs with a smile so bland
And copied all the letters in a big round hand.
I copied all the letters in a hand so free
That now I am the ruler of the Queen's Navee.

We laughed and laughed.

I was convinced that Captain Perry was a *schlemiel* (a simpleton). Lieutenant Burns was a *schlimazel* (someone for whom nothing goes right. A born loser. A Calamity Jane). The Lieutenant of the second platoon, a friend of *schlimazel,* was a nondescript person, more like a *nebbish* (nothing to him). There was another lieutenant of the third platoon, heavy weapons. I had very little contact with him.

So we had a schlemiel, a schlimazel, a nebbish, and a First Sergeant Momzeur running our company. God help us!

With all this, I knew that they held all the aces.

My wife and I decided that she would come out to Colorado Springs, as this was already the middle of May. It would not be long before the division would be alerted for shipment overseas. Since she would have no telephone number to call me, she would send me a letter when she arrived, giving her address and telephone number for me to call. A few days after that ludicrous ordeal, I received a letter from my wife.

I entered Sergeant Momzeur's office to request an unrestricted pass, which was given to soldiers who had wives living in town.

I walked up to the sergeant's desk. He was busily writing (a wonder).

"Yes?" as he looked up at me. He appeared calm enough. "What do you want now?"

"Sergeant," I replied, "my wife has just arrived in town. I would like to have an unrestricted pass to spend time with her."

He stood up, his face became flushed, red with rage, his eyes were bulging again, his mouth frothing. The Goddamn nerve, chutzpah, as it is called. I thought he was going to have an apoplectic fit. Through the froth, he gurgled out, "*Denied!*"

That was it! I turned and started for the door. Spiegel, the company clerk, did his best to keep from choking with laughter. I walked out into the open with the usual expression in mind, "and the hell with you too!" I walked down to the U.S.O., called my wife, and hopped the bus to town, pass or no pass.

She met me at the bus terminal, and welcomed me with hugs and kisses—a delight. Off we went to the boarding house, where I was introduced to the landlady, a lovely woman, who welcomed me. My wife was very excited about the town, a far cry from the closeness of New York City. Colorado Springs was about 5,000 feet elevation. It was a typical western town, open, small buildings, clear, refreshing air, and in the distance the blue range of the Rocky Mountain cliffs, capped by Pikes Peak. It was all very exhilarating, and she loved it. It was an unexpected new experience and she made the most of it. The food in the restaurants was very inexpensive and wholesome. She found the people very friendly, except for one incident which threw her. She told me that when she arrived in town and applied for accommodations at a single family home, showing a notice for "B&B," the woman who came to the door took one look at her and said that she did not rent to foreigners! Imagine the nerve! Here her husband was in a military infantry camp, born and raised in the United States of America, which we regarded as the greatest in the world. Now, I was being trained to fight and die for our country and for that woman, and still we were foreigners. Inconceivable! We paid it no mind. It goes on and on.

As it turned out, her stay lasted for about three weeks, until that day came for preparations to move the division out for shipment overseas.

During these three magnificent weeks, my wife and I managed to get around the environs of Colorado Springs. At camp, the usual program of military activities continued relentlessly, for the most part in the mornings, weekdays, and at times in the afternoon. Whatever free time I could get, I was off to town, pass or no pass, especially on Saturdays, after barracks inspections, overnight and through Sunday, late afternoon.

Saturday afternoons, if the weather was very warm, we managed a swim in the local lake. At dinner, a good steak at the local restaurant. The next morning, Sunday, off to the USO run by both Christian and Jewish families. We were offered a breakfast of orange juice, donuts and coffee, all we could eat. For the afternoon a notice was posted for a "Bar-B-Que" of steak, hamburgers, and frankfurters, to be held in the Garden of the Gods.

Visiting the Garden of the Gods was a religious experience. It was like an open-air cathedral. One could not help but feel like getting down on one's knees and praying. Praise the Lord! The soil was painted in red, which held in its embrace, in the same color, stones and rocks of various dimensions spread out over the land. There were foot paths through this semi-arid plain, complemented by such plants as could grow there. It was said that on Easter mornings, the townspeople would gather there at sunrise for morning services.

Then, we had the occasion to hike up to Manitou Springs for its spring waters, issuing out of a tap for all to take. People arrived with gallon jugs and filled them to their heart's content. We drank our fill, a nice, cool, tasty drink, supposedly good for one's health.

We also went up to the Cave of the Winds, about 11,000 foot elevation . . . we were told. We were offered a lift in a Model-T, as we started to walk up a never ending hill to the top. When we got there, we went to the cave, where we were greeted with the ear-shattering roar of the winds that rushed through the depths of deep tunnels. We were overcome with a sickening case of vertigo, and got out as quickly as possible. This was just too much.

We then proceeded to walk down there. However, *there* was on the other side of the path, which extended about eight feet across a very deep, bottomless chasm, which we had not noticed on the way up while in the car. The path down was very narrow, just about wide enough to take a Model-T. We did not dare look down. The vertigo was almost unbearable and dangerous. We were offered a ride down, but said, "No, thank you very much." Instead, we spread-eagled against the side of the mountain, our faces looking into it, and proceeded down, side-stepping until we cleared the chasm. We were not the only ones doing this. It was quite an experience.

So much for the good times we had. There were others, of course. We made the most of them. It was a pleasant time for my wife; away from New York City and with me, and a very enjoyable interim for me. But it was not to last.

On passing Sergeant Momzeur's office one afternoon, as he stood in the doorway, he addressed me with these inauspicious words, "I know you have been going into town without a leave pass. If the MPs pick you up, I am going to throw the book at you." Meaning, of course, the jailhouse.

I said nothing. I turned my back to him, and walked away. To myself, however, I said, *Just go ahead, you stupid bastard. If you did that, my wife would be off to see our relative, Senator Lehman, who would surely send a stinging memorandum to the Pentagon for a full review of every apparent anti-Semitic harassment of one of his "related" constituents.* The blessings of democracy. A wrathful hullabaloo would descend all the way down the chain of command, to division, then to battalion, and land on the captain's desk, for reply. I cannot imagine that the captain, the schlemiel that he was, could be that much more as to allow the sergeant to carry out his threat. Nothing did happen.

Our training continued as usual until that fateful day, June 6, D-Day when the Allied troops landed in Normandy, France. From that day forward, training was intensified. Passes to town would be limited. I called my wife, and told her that she should be prepared to leave for home, and to let me know what arrangements she had made. I intended to see her off. The best time would be a Sunday—pass or no pass. A few days later, I called her. She made arrangements to leave the coming Sunday, and I told her I would meet her at the train station.

I sneaked a ride, Sunday, into town, and met her at the station. When the train pulled in, it was the saddest day for both of us. She was in tears, and my heart was breaking. I tried to comfort her by telling her it may all be over by the time my outfit sees action. I didn't believe that, but it was better to say something than nothing. Hope is better than pessimism, or so they say.

Back at camp, night maneuvers were increased. I teamed up with Schraeder in supporting each other in whatever the circumstance. About 0300 one night, we (Co. A), on entering a wooded area in pursuit of the enemy (Co. C), inevitably got lost. To hold our territory from counter-attack, we were told to dig foxholes. Schraeder and I located a spot next to a tree that we thought was just right. We started to dig in with our shovels. It was of no use. One inch down, we hit hard shale. We tried digging with our bayonets. That did not help either. We concluded that the only way was with an automatic jackhammer. Imagine going into combat with jackhammers? The racket they would cause as they all took off would wake up the whole neighborhood, including the enemy. After about an hour, we succeeded in forming a resemblance to a hole about two inches deep. We stopped, leaned back on the tree, and laughed and laughed. Schraeder broke out with the next stanza of G&S #III (*HMS Pinafore*):

In serving writs I made such a name
That an articled clerk I soon became
I wore clean collars and a brand new suit
For to pass examinations of the Institute
And that pass examination did so well for me
That now I am the ruler of the Queen's Navee!

Word came along the line to move out to meet the enemy. We did so well in contacting the enemy that we were declared prisoners. We did not even fire a shot. Somehow we fowled up, but it was all good fun and practice. God help us if we ever got caught like this in combat. Well, it was all brought to an end when we shook hands, offered each other cigarettes, and had a good smoke and a good laugh. We walked back to the barracks and off to sleep.

The next morning, Sunday, we were allowed an extra hour of sleep. When we assembled for roll call in the morning, an announcement came over the loud speaker that the maneuver was an overall success. So much for the brilliant military planning and command. We had several such maneuvers, especially for night training, as our division was depicted as night fighters. We trained regardless of weather conditions or physical debilitations. We were the Timber Wolves!

Besides the night maneuvers, we had other practices, as firing on the rifle range, obstacle course training, infiltration crawling under barbed wire as machine guns fired live bullets overhead, bayonet practice, and gas mask drill. The program was intensive and thorough, and the fact that I came through it all without falling apart really built me up physically and even mentally for what I was to experience in combat.

In July, the outfit was alerted. There was a scurry for last minute furloughs, marking items not to be taken overseas, to send to the folks back home, and preparation for our knapsacks and duffel bags to be carried overseas. In the middle of August, the division was moved to Camp Kilmer, New Jersey. On the wall of our barracks, was the usual, KILROY WAS HERE. WHO WAS KILROY?

We were kept at the camp for several days as we were checked on the equipment, clothing, and other accessories that we were to take on board ship. The first weekend, a notice was posted on the USO board that those who had come from the metropolitan area of New York City, could apply for a two-day pass starting Friday night and returning Sunday night. I applied for a pass, but I could never imagine a shaft as malevolent as the one cooked up by Sergeant Momzeur. Instead of the pass, I was posted for guard duty at the USO for Friday and Saturday nights. I was really shook up, and it made no sense to talk to the captain, if I could find him, which I doubted. I tried the chaplain's office. There was no Jewish chaplain. I went to the only one available, a Catholic chaplain.

I expressed myself in no uncertain terms of the malicious intent to deny me the pass. The chaplain said he would do his best. An hour later, he came back and said, "Sorry, the duty was set and I could not do anything for you." I could not believe that. So, the sergeant got in his ultimate cut. I never got over that, not even to this date. To be denied from seeing my wife, father and mother, and other members of my family, before I was to go into combat was as spiteful and humiliating as only the Nazis were capable of doing. Retribution was in the cards.

From Camp Kilmer, we were moved to the point of entry in Brooklyn. We boarded the liberty ship, *Cristobal,* and shipped out. It was not the most pleasant voyage as the T&C manual would describe it.

Our sleeping quarters, two flights down, was arranged with cotton hammocks—three or four layers suspended from the ceiling. It did not take much weight for someone's rear end to be suspended two inches from one's nose. The smell down there with poor circulation of air got so bad that most of us went up on deck with blankets and slept there, if one could sleep.

Seasickness was rampant, and it was a better maneuver to get as close to the rail as possible. Two meals a day, if one could have the appetite to eat. The heat and the humidity below in the dining area with the acrid smell of food cooking, with sweaty cooks in T-shirts, ladling out the food, was as sickening as being above on deck as the ship plowed through the rampant swells of the ocean waves—up and down, up and down, up and down, rolling over and over again. Just looking at the heaving ocean elicited a sympathetic reaction from one's stomach.

Over in the distance, one could see the naval convoy ships. In one respect, a very reassuring presence, but in another, a constant reminder that German submarines could be lurking by . . . not so reassuring.

Such was the routine that was to continue for eleven days. However, by the ninth day, things began to settle somewhat, especially our stomachs. So much for the good. There were paperback books available to be read, and I chose one for its mystery. I did my best not to dwell on past days at Camp Kilmer.

On the eleventh day, we approached what was then known as Utah Beach. We were notified to prepare our duffel bags and other equipment for landing. When the ship stopped some distance from shore, LCT's came up alongside. We handed our bags to, of all people Sergeant Momzeur, who was on the deck of the LCT. We descended on the open-latticed rope netting that acted as ladders. When the LCT filled up, it took off for shore. When it got there, the upright front landing walkway was lowered, and we walked down to the beach with our duffel bags.

We assembled on the beach to await further orders. We stood around smoking, talking, and sometimes walking about to get our land legs back. Just as we began to feel comfortable, a few of the fellows let out exclamations of horror. We turned and saw Sergeant Momzeur suddenly collapse to the ground. He had blacked out. Nobody stirred toward him for the moment. I had my fingers crossed. Schraeder also. I imagine some others had the same reaction. The only ones who approached the fallen sergeant were a few non-coms. They called the officers, who called for the medics. They arrived shortly, put the sergeant on a stretcher, and off they went.

This incident puzzled all of us, and it could not be fathomed. In about an hour or so, a medical officer approached us, and asked if anyone had seen the sergeant in a fight, in an accident, or beating. A negative response. It seemed that the sergeant had blood spots on his spine, a fatal condition. From what we found out later, the sergeant was returned to the state of "Looziana," never to recover, and eventually to die. *Retribution is mine, sayeth the Lord!* So much for that. I had no sympathy for him. I knew and felt deep down, that if he had recovered in France, and had gone all the way with the company, that I would never come out alive. He would have seen to that.

Eventually, army trucks drew up and we ascended. Off we went to the interior where we were settled in an apple orchard outside of a small country town. Apples were still on the trees, and some on the ground. They were as sour as all hell. We were told that these were crushed to make a very potent whiskey known as *Calvados.* Schraeder and I settled into a pup tent for two, furnished by supply. We were given bed rolls. Sanitation was not up as per military manual. Alongside the road there was a stretch of high bushes that could hide us from the view from the road. We dug a series of slit trenches, fifteen feet long, twelve inches wide, two feet deep. The dirt that was dug up was placed alongside the trench. Shovels were dug into the pile of dirt alongside. Also, small sapling branches were set up at intervals to hold a roll of toilet tissue. How does one accommodate himself to the ordeal? Of course, nose to nose, arse to arse, and the devil take hindmost. When it was done, we did whatever had to be done. We took a shovel of dirt from the pile and covered whatever there was on the bottom of the trench. Very sanitary and immaculate. God bless the military! Hot water was made available by the cooks in a large drum and soap suspended alongside. Khaki towels were on the side.

The pleasant side of our settlement were hot breakfasts and hot dinners. A K-ration was issued for lunch. K-rations were made up as a small carton, set up for breakfast, lunch, and dinner. These were made up to be carried during combat. They came in tins, in three different meals, veg-meat, meat and egg, and processed cheese with pieces of bacon enmeshed. With each, there were biscuit crackers, dextrose tablets (for sweetener), soluble coffee packets, fruit bar, tea bags, chocolate bar, bouillon, and lemon juice. The hot meals were very good and satisfying after that sea voyage.

During the daytime, after breakfast, we dressed full field pack and rifle (M-1), shovel and canteen of water, and off we went along the road wherever, walk fifty yards, run fifty yards, two-and-one-half miles here and two-and-one-half miles back. After lunch, French lessons were given by Klein, an ASTP man, a nice fellow, Jewish, of course. Some fellows were detailed to run the Red Ball Express-convoys of food, and all other equipment with troops going toward the front, wherever that might be.

Others relaxed, wrote letters, played volleyball or just simply rested in their tents. In the evenings, some of us walked along the road and paid calls on the peasants as they stood in their doorway. Klein, Schraeder and myself stopped at one humble peasant home. It reminded me of the peasant houses painted by the Barbizon artists, as well as Van Gogh and the Impressionists.

The peasant, was dressed in a very ordinary old shirt, trousers, jacket much for wear, and a beret on his head, with clod hoppers as shoes. As we looked in, we observed a large room, wooden floor and walls, old curtains or drapes hanging on windows, about four of them. The room was lit by kerosene or oil lamps. It was warmed by a very large, fired stove with cooking pots on top. Above the stove, there appeared to be hanging—how, I do not know—bed on which his wife was sleeping.

Klein did most of the talking. I managed to follow well enough as I had studied French in high school and a bit in college. The peasant told us of the hardships he and his wife had endured under German occupation. His horse was confiscated. His wife maintained a small garden and a few chickens. They were hoping to get a pig, if possible, in the market in town. As we noticed the next day, when we walked along the road, he was behind his plow, his wife pulling it on a stretched rope, as an animal would, with a leather strap (harness) encircled around the top of the left shoulder as it moved down along her chest under her right arm to connect with the line to the plow. There, she trudged the damp, sloppy dirt, leaning forward with almost unbearable effort. The ground on which they plowed would be the only source of food they could manage to obtain.

As we stood there talking, the peasant excused himself, went along around the side of the house, unbuttoned his fly, took out his phallus, and urinated right up against the wall. He wiggled his phallus to get a few drops off. He buttoned his fly, returned to our place, and resumed talking, occasionally taking a few puffs from his corncob pipe. So much for the peasant, or others.

We were settled in this place for a couple of weeks. On what appeared to be the last weekend, the outfit was given a bit of respite. Passes were issued to anyone who wanted to go into town. Of course, everybody knew why anyone would want to go into town—booze and couchy-couchy women. Condoms were issued. The next morning, most of them stalked back, inebriated, soused, drunk, if you will, half-blind (momentarily) from drinking that very powerful *Elixir d'Amour,* known as *Calvados.*

Not for me, nor for Schraeder. We had many discussions as we prepared our bedrolls for sleep. He told me he was Catholic, which I already knew, and that he had fallen out with his family as he refused to practice the religion. He had no particular liking for the Catholic Church, nor for the priests. In consideration of the unholy and horrendous practices throughout the 2,000 years of history, he would not square them with its teachings.

That Sunday was a day of rest to do as we pleased. In the afternoon, some of the guys hooked a line attached to two trees down below the road on level ground, and played volleyball. I watched the game from the road. As I stood there, I spied the captain and his three lieutenants on my right from the corner of my eye as they were walking in my direction.

As they approached, I turned to them and saluted; the captain acknowledged. He then said, "Come along with us, Hanish, I would like to talk to you." Much to my astonishment. *What now?*

I turned toward them as they kept walking, bringing up the rear. When we got to their sleeping quarters—a small furnished house, we entered. The captain sat on his bed. I came up before him. "At ease," came the call. I relaxed.

The captain then went on with what appeared to be an apologetic declaration. "I would like to tell you," he continued, "that we intend to forget what was said and what occurred back in Camp Carson concerning Senator Lehman's request for an explanation on the withdrawal of your corporal's rating. My reply and statement to you and him were, I feel now, completely out of order. So, we will let bygones be bygones." This is not verbatim, but the gist is there. "Do you have anything to say?"

I replied, "Thank you very much, Sir. I appreciate your speaking to me."

With that, he dismissed me. I saluted, made an about face, and walked to the door, and out, in a very soldierly fashion.

When I got outside into the fresh air, I remarked to myself in a very low whisper, "Now, what the hell was that all about?" I never did take him seriously then, not that schlemiel. But I did not forget nor forgive. Not after he permitted that Sergeant Momzeur to harass me, and to deny me a pass to visit my wife at Camp Carson, and to deny me an overnight pass to see my wife and family at Camp Kilmer. And also, the way the captain denigrated my character and ability as a soldier in his reply to the senator. It also became part of my record, not that it really mattered. As I mentioned before, I had no intention to rise in the ranks. I was damned at Camp Carson, and resurrected before combat, like a good Christian. Oh, but I was not a Christian. I was Jewish, like Christ. Now I was beginning to understand what it was all about!

This was about October. The days were balmy and serene, but damp. Training was always in session. Some units were called upon to run the Redball Express transportation to Granville, the Cherbourg-Paris pipeline. Others were assigned to various guard duty functions.

About the middle of October, the division was assembled in the vicinity of Barneville, where we boarded the notorious forty and eights (forty men and eight horses to a car). The small, creaky cars would hardly accommodate forty men or even thirty, much less eight horses. They were hot, stuffy and stifling, even with the doors open. The lavatories were outside in the open along the tracks when the train stopped periodically. We stopped in Paris for a short while, but remained at the station. We then took another train to Vilvoorde, Belgium.

Quoting from the account published of our experience in Belgium, "When the troops detrained at Vilvoorde, the Belgians flocked to the trains with apples, pears, and coffee, to welcome the first American troops to come to their city. The children in groups at street corners cheered and waved flags, as the trucks careened by with loads of soldiers on their way to the next assembly area." This assembly area was adjacent to hospital towns and cities. We set up our pup tents and made our slit trenches. The cooks set up to prepare hot meals.

On Saturday, we were notified that this would be the last weekend in this area before entering combat. A night pass was offered to anyone who wished to go into town. Schraeder came up to me and said, "I'm going into town to get laid." He was a virgin, you know, and he was going to experience this act of heavenly love . . . even with a prostitute.

Not for me. I could not see myself ending up with a bad case of V.D. while trying to negotiate myself through a hail of bullets and bombs all around. Besides, I had no liking for such a precarious, momentary expenditure of delirious delight with some woman who had not the slightest interest nor concern for me.

"OK," I replied, "don't forget to ask the first sergeant for a prophylactic kit, and make sure you use it. Good luck and happy returns. If you can find some nice chick who's willing to take you around the world, for the evening, go for it."

That evening after supper, the men were loaded onto trucks, and off they went into town. I returned to our tent for a lie down, as the British would say. In short time, I was off to sleep.

The next morning, I was up early. I looked over to Schraeder's bed roll, and found it was not slept in. I figured maybe he was lucky to have found that chick. I put on my shoes, and walked over to the first sergeant's high top tent. He was at his desk (of sorts).

"Good morning, Sarge," I said. "I noticed that Schraeder had not returned. Do you know if he stayed in town?"

The sergeant shook his head. "I will let you know if I hear anything."

I left for the chow line. I felt very uneasy about Schraeder. I had the inner feeling that something was wrong.

As I started back to my tent after eating breakfast, one of the fellows accosted me, and inquired, "Are you Hanish?"

I replied I was.

"Sergeant wants to talk to you."

"OK, thanks."

There again, I had that queasy feeling. Something is wrong, I sensed. I walked over to the sergeant's tent and stood in front of his desk anxiously. He looked up at me and sadly said, "I have bad news for you. Schraeder was *killed* by one of our trucks as it was returning from town. It seems that for some reason, Schraeder decided to walk back. You know the trucks do not put their headlights on in a blackout area."

I looked at the sergeant in utter disbelief. "I don't understand this," I said. "We're not even in combat and he's already dead? He didn't even have the honor of being killed in combat like a hero! What irony!" I thanked the sergeant, and walked back to the tent in utter dismay.

It is sung to the moon
By a love-lorn loon,
Who fled from the mocking throng, O.
It's the song of a merryman, moping mum
Whose soul was sad, and whose glance was glum
Who supped no sup and craved no crumb
As he sighed for the love of a ladye.
—G&S, *The Yeoman of the Guard*

Schraeder's personal items and duffel bag were picked up. I couldn't get over his death. It was the first of many casualties that I was to witness. The first usually is the hardest to take. I lost a buddy. It would have made things much easier had he been with me in combat. But it's true as the ca-

65

sualties mounted, the inner-psyche becomes ensealed in a hard crust for its own sake and survival. I became a veteran.*C'est la guerre, mon ami!*

Sunday, morning, the day before we were to enter into combat, we were ordered to lay out our knapsack to check that we had all of our necessities. Our rifles (M-1) were examined for a clean bore and operation. We were also issued ammunition, a canteen for water, first-aid kit, bayonet, and a small, folding shovel, all to be attached to our webbed belts in separate pouches, except for the shovel, which we attached to our knapsack.

In the afternoon, we were treated to words of caution and enlightenment on entering combat. The lecture was given by a colonel of WWI vintage. He was about 50-ish, tall, slim, and carried an officer's baton, which he waved about to emphasize his words. The most memorable part of his lecture that I came away with was the following (not verbatim, just the gist):

"You are here, and going into combat. There is no way out without facing the enemy. He is out to kill you, so if you want to survive, you have to kill him first. That's the bottom line."

So, with such an uplifting sermon, which was to make us feel so much better, he continued on, telling us of some of his experiences. As he droned on, I kept thinking of Schraeder. How would he have taken all this? In memory, I recalled the time he entered the doorway of our barracks, and recited this stanza from G&S, *The Pirates of Penzance.*

I am the very model of a modern major general,
I've information vegetable, animal, and mineral
I know the Kings of England, and I quote the fights historical
From Marathon to Waterloo (?) categorical.
I'm very well acquainted too with matters mathematical
I understand equations, both the single and quadratical,
About biennial theorem I'm teeming with a lot of news—
With many cheerful facts about the square of the hypotenuse.
I'm very good at integral and differential calculus
I know the scientific name of animalcules
In short, in matters vegetable, animal and mineral
I am the very model of a modern major general.

The rest of the afternoon, I wrote letters to those back home. There would be not much time afterwards. I gave no hint of what was to take place the next morning. Very little was said or to talk about among the fellows. I did miss Schraeder. It would have been good to share our thoughts, and to arrange a way of looking out for each other. But that was water under the bridge. No sense of dwelling over this. *C'est fini!*

In the evening, we had our last supper. We were then issued three packets of K-rations. I put these into my knapsack, I took my shoes off, and slid them into my sleeping bag. It took a while before I went off to sleep. What the hell! It's up to the gods, or as I was to feel later . . . it's up to my fate! I came to believe later that each person is born with his fate already subscribed in the Book of Life. A person would never know *that* until that fateful day, when the truth would be revealed.

When I attended college and took Philosophy 101, a study of the ancient Greek philosophers, I was very much taken with the *Meditations* of the Emperor Marcus Aurelius, the Stoic. His thoughts soothed my troubled psyche in the thirties when the world, and the troubles of my parents, when it seemed that everything was going awry. I was nurtured into a feeling of inner-calmness that helped me to remain steady in those tragic and unexpected, sorrowful events that befell those close to me, and those of the rusted world around me.

VI
Combat

From where we were in the assembly area, we were awakened in the early, dark morning, packed our gear, and proceeded to move silently through the thickly forested area to meet the British Forty-Ninth Division. We were now attached to General Montgomery's field division. At first, we were served a hot breakfast of pork chops (of all things), potatoes, beans, and coffee. This was most welcome, as the air was damp and cold. We cleaned our mess kits and cups in a large drum of hot water, dried them with towels that hung from a branch. Before we could fold the mess kits and cups for packing, we were ordered to move into an open clearing, with our mess kits and cups dangling from our belts. They raised such a racket, one could hear it all the way to Berlin, as could the Germans probably ensconced in the trees ahead of us.

None of us were in any way aware of what was really going to happen, or happening, for that matter. Neither did we have any orientation as to what to expect. We just moved forward in parallel lines stretched from left to right. I was in the third line. The sky was clear and sharp. The stars blinked quietly as if in amazement at what they were witnessing. The moon shone brightly on our right, innocently.

Suddenly, the air was rent with the repeated staccato sounds of machine gunfire. Up above our field of vision, bullets kept streaming toward us and every tenth one (it seemed that way) was lit up like fireflies. The Germans had been waiting for us, somewhere in front in a grove of trees, or was it above ground among the trees. It seemed that the Germans had a perfect view of us as we moved forward.

A cry went up! "The captain is killed!" He got a bullet in the helmet. One fellow remarked to me, "If you see the tracers, you're alive. If not, you're dead." Thank God, I could still see them. Now that the captain was dead, where was Lt. Schlimazel and Nebbish? Probably having nervous breakdowns. They followed in the rear with revolvers drawn. We had no leader.

As we moved along the field, we came across the first obstacle—a barbed wire fence. On my left, I notice one of our men, an ASTP young fellow hanging over the wire, quite dead, his right eyeball was hanging from its socket. There were a couple of others on my right, also hanging over the wire, quite dead also. I could only imagine that they had tried to go over the wire which elevated them in line of fire. It would have been better if supply had issued wire cutters. But that was neither here nor there. I was not going over the wire, to be sure. I tried going underneath the bottom line—there were two lines altogether, but there was no room to get myself and pack under. Instead, I raised the butt of my rifle and slammed down on the wire next to the staple on the post. I was joined by several others. We got the wire down to the ground, and stepped on the lower wire without much difficulty. We moved forward. All this time, I was moving in a semi-crouched position.

We proceeded along the open ground, the tracers still flying above us. There were several men stretched out on the ground, some dead, some groaning in a low voice for the medics. Then again, another stretch of barbed wire, but this time completely down, both lines. We stepped over the wires, and ran slap into rows of stretched out bodies lying alongside each other, heads facing the trees in front, quite alive but still. The machine gunfire was coming through the forest opening straight at us. There was nothing to do but lie still, and hope that some other units on our flanks would overwhelm the German machine gunners. It seemed that we had lost our command. The captain was dead, and our platoon lieutenants were somewhere in the rear, probably momentarily shell shocked.

Our position was untenable. The Germans, much more experienced, had ambushed us into a trap. They started to pummel us with mortar fire. The war had been going on for four years, and nowhere in our training manuals was there ever mentioned the tactics used by the Germans to embroil their enemy into a mortar fiasco. This tactic was used repeatedly throughout our campaigns. After the war, writers of the campaigns in Europe stated that the greatest number of casualties among American soldiers were due to mortar fire.

Our platoon Sergeant Manners took command. He stood up on the right edge of the group, and yelled, "Leave your knapsacks behind, and take everything else, including shovels, with you. Roll over to your right into the patch of trees, and dig in."

We did as we were told, and rolled over rapidly into the wooded area. I was joined by Klein. We were beginning to match each other. Others in twos and threes, scattered about, and started to dig in furiously. It didn't take much time to dig down three or four feet. We soon found that the soil in Holland was soft and damp. It was not long before water seeped up from the bottom, and it wasn't long before you found your feet and then your legs up to the knees soaked in water. But we had to do with it.

Then came the mortar shells, which followed us to this new area, hitting the tree tops and exploding above us, showering us with sharp, zinging shrapnel chunks. We hastily grabbed the fallen branches, which still held dried leaves, and dragged them over to cover us. We did this from the confines of our hole, reaching out each time to pull over a fallen branch. It was not the best cover to have, since there were many exposed spots. But it was the best we could do.

The explosions were filling the air with flying pieces of shrapnel in every direction, and coming down on us with tremendous force. With each explosion, more branches came tumbling down. We just simply extended our arms to those that fell near us, and dragged them over the ones already in place over our heads. This procedure was followed by all of the other groups, but it offered only a modicum of protection. Some shrapnel fell through, others came zinging through at tremendous speed. In the next hole, a cry went up hysterically, "Jimmy is hit! Jimmy is hit!" Jimmy was an American Indian, who buddied up with a couple of southerners. It didn't take long before cries went up all over the area calling for medics.

It didn't take long for the firing to start easing up, but it was still not over. On looking through the branches over our heads, I noticed the colonel of WWI vintage being supported by two non-coms, his right and left arms over the shoulders of the non-coms as he walked out of the woods into the clearing, in spite of an occasional explosion overhead. We were later told that the colonel had sustained shrapnel wounds in both of his knees. He was lucky. *Hors de Combat.*

Klein finally got his million dollar wound. A piece of shrapnel came zinging through, and cut his left thigh. It was a deep gash, and he was moaning in pain. I took his first-aid kit from the pouch hanging from his belt in back of his waist. I opened it, and grabbed the small sealed envelope of sulfa powder which I spread over the bleeding wound. I then applied a thick gauze pad over it, which I taped down with bandage adhesive. There wasn't much I could do. I knew we had to get out of this hole as soon as possible. The explosions were letting up. I couldn't take a chance on supporting him through the woods. He was heavier than I was, and we certainly would run the risk of both of us getting hit.

I decided to make a run for it into the clearing I had noticed before. It would make more sense to get the medics to him. As soon as I thought I could make it, I told Klein that I was going to get the medics. I crawled out of the hole, dragged some more fallen branch which I placed over the hole, and took off—in a wild dash. When I cleared the woods, right outside, I noticed three guys sitting in a foxhole, manning a machine gun. *What the hell were they doing there* I wondered.

The sun was shining in the warm air. It was mid-morning, I gathered. It was all so peaceful and calm. There was a group of soldiers on a mound further along, standing about, smoking, without a care in the world, talking of our great "adventure," and glad to be alive. I spied the medics with their stretchers, also standing about. I went up to them and exclaimed that there were wounded men in the foxholes in that patch of woods, that they were in pretty bad shape! I spoke with an apprehensive tone of voice that conveyed a matter of life and death. Two sets of medics took off on the run. It had its effect.

Klein looked me up in Camp Kilmer when the outfit returned to the States. I was asleep in the barracks. He came up to me, and shook me out of my trance. "Howdy," he said to me in as jocular mood as can be. I was not in a jocular mood. I was fatigued out, half-asleep, with a time lag that I did not as yet recover. I resented his being so jocular, but I was glad to see him.

"What happened to you?" I asked.

He had a story that I could only wish on myself. He was taken to England, hospitalized for about two weeks, and then convalesced accompanied by two of the most beautiful chicks (nurses) as they walked him around the grounds. As an ASTP man, the Army officials kept him as a clerk in an HQ outfit, the lucky stiff!

So much for Klein. I lost track of him once we were discharged.

Back to reality. I was still up on the mound with the others, smoking and talking. In time, the word came down to return to the field to pick up our gear. The firing had completely stopped. We were told that the Germans were retreating. We got our stuff, and then assembled in walking formation by platoon, company, and regiment. There weren't too many left to continue, perhaps about 60 percent.

We started on a long, arduous trek. The Germans were retreating so fast it called for maximum effort to keep up with them. I didn't know it then, but in time, we learned that the Germans were heading for a river to cross. I learned, in time, that this procedure was their favorite tactic of retreat—head for a river to cross, heading East, set up a defense line, and counterattack as we attempted to cross. That would explain why we were in such rush to catch up with the Germans before they made it.

Only in experience, costly as such, did we learn something of the Germans' tactics. First, to get us in an open clearing, then machine gun us to lie low, and then pulverize us with mortar fire. As we advanced, it almost seemed that our top officers were not cognizant of these tactics, as we were constantly caught in these devastating situations, time and again. These tactics resulted in most of our casualties. They cost us dearly.

In time, we learned that the Germans were heading for the Mark River further east. Rest stops were infrequent. We had very few chances to eat, even our K-rations. We managed, at times, to chew on chocolate and fruit bars that were in the rations. Sometimes, we had the good fortune to open one of the cans, especially cheese with bacon (which I preferred), that we chewed on the road as we walked and walked, and washed down with swigs of water from our canteens.

Fighting in Holland was an experience all by itself. The terrain presented tremendous obstacles. It was cluttered with canals and dikes, flat and wet with water lingering just below the surface of the soil. Within a few minutes, every foxhole became a muddy bathtub!

The lack of sleep from about three o'clock in the morning since going into combat was beginning to take its toll, not only for me, but for all the others. As we kept walking (somewhat dragging ourselves), word came down that there were Germans in a patch of woods over to the left beyond some open ground. The order was given to move in. We formed a thin line on the slope off the road, laying against it with our heads and rifles above, awaiting the enemy. I had not as yet attained the machismo of a veteran. I felt my head wanting to sink downward through my neck and into my chest—a typical reaction. Was I scared? Of course! Who wouldn't be?! Nothing happened.

"Everybody up!" came the order. "Move across the field!" I clambered up the slope, and started to move across the open field toward the woods, in a parallel straight line across, with plenty of space between each of us. Much to my surprise, Schlimazel and Nebbish were moving along with us in line, muttering to themselves as usual. Where the hell did *they* come from?

A new tactic—to us, anyway—was brought into play, called a rolling barrage. At the end of the line to our right, there was an artillery observer calling the shots to the artillery battery somewhere in back of us. Artillery shells were beginning to fall and explode about forty to fifty feet in front of us. We were not affected by them, but we had our fingers crossed.

There was no enemy fire directed at us. I walked cautiously, always maintaining my position in line, and as usual, crouched down. Halfway there, we noticed a trench running parallel in front of the patch of woods. It appeared to be unoccupied, and we made a run for it. As we got to it, we jumped in bellyside against the inner slope. We slowly raised our heads and looked across. Holy Moses! A sight to behold!

About three feet in front of us, there were two mounds side by side and parallel to the trench, of packed earth, the length of a man. The heads were exposed, wearing knitted head gear; eyes, nose and lips exposed, dead of course—it could hardly be otherwise. Small crosses, made of branch twigs, were implanted close to the heads. I had the impression that under the earthy cover their arms were crossed in Teutonic fashion as observed on fully sculptured stone in knight's armor on covers of the burial sarcophaguses displayed in museums.

I slid down into the trench, turned on my back, looked at the guy on my left and said, "Now I have seen everything." He nodded. I reached into my pocket, and took out an almost empty pack of cigarettes. I offered one to the fellow, who took it, and we both lit up, with a sigh of relief on the first puff. We had no problem with getting cigarettes. They were readily obtained from supply. All of this was very interesting. In all of my Social Science classes, we never did go into the funeral practices of peoples around the globe.

It didn't take long before the call came up to return to the road. We continued walking. On the way, we picked up much needed K-rations and water from supply trucks along the road. We were given additional chores, in small groups, of checking for German soldiers who may have strayed, or positioned themselves in small villages along the road, or in some cases, small villages inland from the road. We were also required to check elevated slopes (small hills) astride the road, and at times to walk along the ridges. There weren't too many of these hills since Holland was essentially flat.

In time, it was starting to get dark early, and as we moved forward, slower and slower, my legs began to feel like posts of lumber. They were protesting the order to move! No sleep for the last fifteen hours was beginning to take its toll. I was learning the trick, so far, of trying to nap while walking, as so many others did. We walked only half conscious, one might say, and lost track of time. If only they would call a halt, and let some other chaps chase the Germans! There were a few men laying on the side of the road, completely out and asleep, it seemed.

It was perhaps some time after midnight, pitch black. The stars were shining brightly, and as usual, completely indifferent to my woes. And so it happened that the Great Sages of G-2, I&I (Information and Intelligence) sent word down the line "Nothing in front of us, keep going!" About half an hour later, the silence was broken with the booming of artillery in front of us. Then they came, sturdy messengers of welcome, screaming like the banshees (or perhaps the Valkyries) of a Wagnerian opera. The big-chested, broad-bodied Aryan heroines in chest plates, and winged helmet, screaming at the top of their lungs like the meemies that came down on us with thunderous claps: *E-E-E-E-E-keplow! E-E-E-E-E-keplow!* Wagner, so beloved by Hitler, his Nazi murderers, German fascists, and as well as by a majority of the German population, chose the Norse, Teutonic myths as his subject matter for his operas. It was through these myths that Hitler tried to inculcate in the minds and breasts of the German people and of his troops, that it was better to die a hero's death on the battlefield than to live out a Christian life of turning the other cheek in a meaningless effort to achieve happiness into a decrepit old age. Death on the battlefield was rewarded by a place in the Halls of Odin, in Valhalla.

We scrambled to get off the road. Immediately to our left, a barbed-wire fence once again. We slammed down with the butts of our rifles, ripped the staples off the wire from the posts, onto the ground, and started to dig into the earth for a foxhole, three of us. Two feet down, then three feet, water began to seep up. The hell with it! Two guys started to pull up the posts, three of them. I moved over to the saplings nearby, and proceeded to chop off branches, with dried leaves still on, with my bayonet. It didn't take long to get a good supply. I dragged them over to the foxhole, and covered the three posts. I slid through an opening, dragging a branch with me to cover the spot above me.

We settled down. We felt we could come out OK, as long as a direct hit did not befall us. Then of course we could be known as MIAs, or unknown soldiers. What the hell! If only I could sleep!

So much for G-2. I never trusted them again. Then some calls for the medics went up.

So, while lying in that damp foxhole, slowly forming itself into a bathtub, in my mind's eye I caught a glimpse of Schraeder, that good fellow, sounding off with another stanza from *HMS Pinafore*:

In serving writs, I made such a name
That an articled clerk I soon became.
I wore clean collars and a brand new suit
For to pass examinations of the Institute,
And that pass examination did so well for me,
That now I am the ruler of the Queens Navee.

Some time passed before shelling subsided. How long I could not fig-ure. I only knew that the seeping water was wetting us up to our waists. Finally, the call came to leave the foxholes, and to continue forward on the road. It is amazing that in spite of my lack of sleep and fatigue and of hav-ing the feeling that I just about had it, that I could have reacted with such energy when the shelling started. It only demonstrates how nature fur-nishes the necessary hormones in the human animal, like all others to pre-pare it for flight when confronted with danger. This energized effect didn't last long.

Lieutenant Schlimazel and Nebbish didn't show up. Instead, a tall slim Lieutenant came up to the head of our lines. I never saw him before. Must be a repot depot, or one of those ninety day wonders. Suddenly, we found ourselves walking into a pea-soup fog, as the dawn was breaking. We could scarcely see beyond six feet in front of us. Over on our left, we noticed a thick, bluish haze, indicating water—the River Mark that was previously mentioned. We continued walking, following the Lieutenant, and wondering if he knew where he was going. He stopped occasionally to get his bearings. We had all we could do to keep from walking into each other.

Finally, we came up to what appeared as an outline of a farm house over to our left, alongside of which were tall, cone-shaped haystacks nearer to the road. The lieutenant stopped, and we did as well, and said, "Stay here for the moment. I am going back to see what's going on."

He walked off, and we waited, and waited. About a half hour later, he did not return. As a matter of fact, he never returned. And so, we all felt the hell with it, and scampered off toward the farm house.

I chose the nearest haystack. I was almost falling off my feet for lack of sleep. I had enough! I was going to take a nap, come what may! I re-leased my shovel from its holder, and dug in as wide a berth as I could manage. I burrowed myself in head first, helmet and all. I made sure I was completely covered, with enough passage to allow the air in. I fell promptly to sleep, Rip Van Winkle style.

I had no idea how long I had slept. It must have been several hours. As I wiggled myself out, I heard what appeared to be mortar shells bursting about, and a mortar being fired nearby. Pieces of shrapnel were dropping aimlessly all around. I dropped to the ground, cradled my rifle in my arms, looked over to the farm house on my left, where I noticed some of the guys in twos and threes running for the door of the farm house. As they hit the door and fell in, a German mortar shell dropped behind them. I looked over to my right and noticed a tree with dry foliage still on. Just beyond, there was a group of soldiers and a Lieutenant whom I figured to be an engineer firing mortar shells across the river. I somehow surmised that they were firing a mortar and shells left behind by the Germans in their haste to get across the river. I could never understand why the Germans did not shell them.

Anyway, I crawled over to the tree, dug a shallow foxhole, water and all, just to observe the farm house. I had to relieve myself, but tried to hold out. It didn't take long before I noticed that the number of men making a run for the farm house began to slacken. I also noticed that these fellows did not have their field packs on, nor were they carrying rifles. As the time intervals extended, I decided to make a run for it as soon as a couple guys dived into the doorway, accompanied by a mortar shell on their tails. I waited a few moments, and decided to take off. I got out of the hole, set myself for a fifty-yard dash, and took off. When I got to the door, I fell into it with my left shoulder, almost losing my balance. A mortar shell burst outside, fortunately for me the door had closed. To hell with you, too!

I walked in nonchalantly, a bit of bravado. Over to the right, there was a large room filled with fellows talking. It must be the kitchen as there was a very large stove all fired with warmth and smoke. The fellows had strung lines across the room over the stove from which they hung their wet khaki shirts, trousers, socks, and underwear, combat boots on the ground near the stove. Along a wooden table that stretched across the room near the door, with its occupied wooden chairs in disarray, also were set near the stove. The fellows were eating out of the K-ration cans. They had hot coffee to drink, or were chewing away on chocolate bars. They were amply covered with Army blankets. I assumed all this was provided by the group from my platoon that ran into the farm house from the road.

I continued walking along the center of the barn toward the rear. The Dutch peasants tended to keep both house and barn as one unit. On my right, there were a couple of guys snoring on top of a stack of loose hay that reached up to the roof. On my left, a lonely, neglected cow was mooing for

76

attention. In the middle of the floor, a cellar door was ajar, and I heard children crying below. As I looked down, I noticed the farmer, his wife, and two children who couldn't contain their tears.

I walked around the cellar door to the rear, and found another room there. A group of men were sitting around a long table, having a hot discussion about what, I cared not. They were quite dry, and enjoying their K-rations. I walked across the room (nobody took notice of me), and opened the door to the backyard. I relieved myself right up against the wall, French style. So much for that. I was much relieved.

I walked back to the kitchen. What happened, I wondered? I approached Pomeroy, who was wrapped in a blanket, a South Carolinian, sergeant of the Second Platoon. He was a very pleasant fellow back in the States. I didn't have much to do with him, but he was nice enough without hangups.

"What happened?" I asked him. Below is a long, tragic story in so many words.

In the foggy dew of early morning, his platoon and those behind of Companies A and B, were lined up along the shore of the river, on which long boats were stationed. They were ordered to get into them, so many to a boat, and to shove off across the river. They weren't sure as to the width of the river, but estimated it to be about fifty feet. They paddled across until they hit shore, scrambled out and up the slope, which was not too steep. They were told to move inland about fifty feet and to dig foxholes. Some were lucky to get to a few houses.

Their objective was to establish a bridge head and to hold fast until the rest of the division could get across on pontoon bridges. Well, no sooner did they settle down, than the fog lifted. They were met with a withering counterattack, machine gun fire and mortar shells bursting all over, and then the worst of it all, *tanks!* For a soldier facing the monster of a tank (a veritable dinosaur), spewing forth machine gun bullets, and coming at him with no other intention than to smash him to a scrambled egg, holy Jesus! Try to stop it with rifle bullets!

This was not all. Alongside of the tanks were German infantry soldiers. What to do? Pray to Jesus and to God and hope for deliverance. Nonsense! The only thing to do is either jump up and shout *Kamerade* (I surrender), or take off for the river. Some of them did. Some didn't make it. They were shot anyway. They left everything behind and jumped into the river, and swam back to the safety of our lines. That accounted for all the scurrying toward the barn door, and for the wet clothing hanging over the kitchen stove. Boy, was I lucky!

I commiserated with Sergeant Pomeroy, and offered him a spare K-ration and cigarette. I opened my one remaining K-ration, and took it all in; bacon and cheese in solid form, hard biscuit and a swig of water from my canteen. Then, a bar of chocolate, a cigarette, and waited until the hullabaloo calmed down.

About two hours later, the order came down to withdraw to the rear, as it turned out, about two or three miles from the river. The men took their damp clothing, partially dried, dressed, and took positions in lines on both sides of the road, and off we trudged away from the river. About two miles back, we found ourselves at an open, grassy field, where we spied Sergeant Ginelli propped up behind some wooden crates, which he was using as a desk. He was keeping records of those who showed up, and those that didn't. We were signed in, and notified to make ourselves at home. He pointed to a stack of cardboard boxes over to his right, and told us to help ourselves.

We walked over to the stack of boxes, and read the printout, C-rations. We immediately tore open the lids of the boxes, and found to our astonishment and glee, one-pound cans of C-rations, that came in ten edible provisions. There were meat and beans, meat and vegetable stew, spaghetti and meatballs, ham, egg and potatoes, meat and noodles, frankfurter and beans, pork and beans, ham and lima beans, corned-beef hash, and beef ravioli. Gourmet ecstasy in Nirvana! This was the first time that we ever knew of or saw them, never to see them again. This was a happy interlude, more than enough for the fifteen left of our group.

We dug our foxholes, three men in each, but it didn't take long before we got water seepage. I noticed that in a not-too-distant area, roofing of houses, which would indicate, probably, a small village. We approached the sergeant with my suggestion that we might obtain a few bales of hay, if available. We figured it would insulate the foxholes against water seepage. He thought it was a good idea, and suggested that we take a few cans of C-rations with us. We also had some spare sugar and coffee packets to add to our C-rations. The three of us packed three cans each, and took off. We walked about one-half mile before approaching the village, which seemed to be quite substantial.

We stopped at the nearest barn and entered. There were Dutch farmers standing and talking. We also noticed that there were stacks of baled hay on the side against the walls. We approached the men, who seemed surprised at seeing American soldiers entering the barn. I greeted them, and tried my best in a mix of English and pidgin Yiddish in obtaining some bales of hay. My efforts were laughable. They responded in perfectly good English, "OK."

We asked for three bales of hay, if available, and offered our cans of C-rations, coffee, and sugar in return. No problem. It didn't take long before they loaded three bales of hay on one of their wagons, to which they hitched two horses. They were lucky they still had them. When finished, we hopped on and sat down next to the hay. Two farmers drove along with us for the ride.

When we got to our rest camp, the hay was unloaded, the wire bindings were cut, and with our thanks, the farmers took off. We dragged as much hay as needed to feather our nest. Each group pitched in for themselves. Once furnished, we gathered up as many cans of C-rations, of all varieties, as we could carry to our hole, where we lined them up in the front.

We were famished, so we set to. We decided to open three different foods to be heated and shared. We all had small, folding trivets, which we spread, exposing a small tray in the middle. We all had small round pellets that lit up to furnish heat when fired by a match. We opened the cans with a makeshift small folding metal can opener, furnished in our K-rations. We placed the cans on the trivets and fired the pellets; spaghetti and meatballs, frankfurters and beans, ham and lima beans, gourmand meals! Our mouths watered at the aromas. What glee! What ecstasy! What good fortune! What more could one want!

When the food started to simmer, we thought it time to eat. We opened our mess kits, took out our metal forks and spoons, and proceeded to dish out the contents, one third each as best we could. That done, we slid down our little nest, our backs to the sides, and went to town. A real gourmet treat! Couldn't ask for anything better. So, it went on for two more days. We ate well, nested and slept as best we could. In time, more stragglers joined us.

On the third day, the battalion commander, Major, assembled what was left of his command, about eighty men—a shambles—out on the road near the old camp. He stood up on a wooden crate, and spoke at length on what a fine job we had all done, and how much was accomplished, and etc., etc. etc. I am not too sure of how proud the men felt, only each of us was glad to have survived. Our replaced Lieutenant never showed up.

IV—*HMS Pinafore*:

Of legal knowledge I acquired such a grip
That they took me into the partnership—
And that partnership I ween
Was the only ship I ever had seen.
And that kind of ship so suited me
That now I am the Ruler of the Queen's Navee.

On the third day, Lieutenant Schlimazel and Nebbish showed up. Where the hell had they been? We could very well do without them. They promptly preempted our little nest with nary a word. The three of us split up and each joined another group in their nest.

On that night, our artillery opened up a barrage of shell fire across the river. It was so strong that our whole area shook as if hit by an earthquake. This went on all night . . . no sleep. Schlimazel and Nebbish were talking to each other aloud. They seemed to be going nuts. They kept saying that they were not going to be shot from behind, over and over again. A clear case of paranoia. I was sure that sooner or later they would both really crack up. Call it battle fatigue. It would be good riddance, *hors de combat.*

The next morning, we were on the move for another crossing of the river. The artillery had stopped. On reaching the shore, we found a newly constructed pontoon bridge over the river. Some units had already crossed and established a bridge head on the other side. We were told that we were attached to Company B under the command of Captain I. Garino, which had also been depleted. Captain Garino turned out to be a humane, competent officer, an Italian from one of the northern cities. No hangups or prejudices of any kind.

As we waited near the bridge to go across, three of the characters of the old group from my company approached me with the most ridiculous declarations of craven rationalizations I have ever heard. "No, no, no! They were not going to get themselves killed for the Jews." I looked at them with astonishment. If one had the imaginary sight to see above my helmet, he would see a big question mark hovering. They continued.

"The Jews cause all our troubles!" (Shades of Father Coughlin and Charles Lindbergh.) The international Jewish financiers with their greed to corner the wealth of the world caused the Depression, and are raking as much money from the war industries as they could gather. President Roosevelt was their puppet because of all the money they gave toward his campaign finances. They involved the United States in this war against Hitler, who was fighting to destroy communism, and to save the Jews, the real troublemakers. The Jews were "Christ killers," and deserved everything they got from the Nazis. They were not going to fight for the Jews and get themselves killed.

Without much ado, they turned around and took off to the rear as fast as they could go, away from the bridge. I never saw them again. I could not help feeling, a well established fact, that there was a pervasive and insidious anti-Jewish sentiment that permeated the United States, especially in the Christian South.

The few that remained of our company crossed over the bridge and moved without any reaction from the Germans. The way further into Holland was clear. We moved rapidly. In groups of four or five, we deviated off the road to check the Dutch homes and barns for German stragglers. None were found.

In one farm house we rested at about noon. Some of us went through the house to the rear courtyard of sorts with a shed that encompassed the open court in a U-shape. Six of us took seats on extended benches from the wall along the shed, with one hanging wooden shade. It was drizzling as usual; cold and damp. We had our raincoats on. In the middle of the yard was a putrid, smelly compost of straw and manure.

As we were thinking of opening a K-ration, two guys came out of the house, each carrying a small cardboard box. They called my name for identification. I answered and I was given both boxes. I opened both boxes, sent by Katz's Delicatessen on Houston Street, Manhattan, New York City, as ordered by my good wife. I decided that three of us could share one box, and the other I gave to the three that were seated separately alongside. No sense in carrying any of these except the candles. Although the salami was a bit smelly, it was still edible, fortunately. We went to town with it. I divided it into thirds with my bayonet, four inches each, and that was that! Everything else was divided three ways.

As we sat there munching away at our glorious repast, we found ourselves staring across the yard about twelve feet at two overblown draught horses, laying on their left sides together—*quite dead.* They were gigantic. Their legs jutted out stiffly from their bodies in midair, their behinds facing us. Extending from their anal orifices (assholes, in the vernacular) were large balloon-like shapes of their rectal intestines, about twelve inches in diameter. One of the fellows leaned over to my left ear, and whispered, "Gas, you know." I was wondering, were they to explode right then and there, while we were sitting there, POW! There goes Western Civiliza-

81

tion, full of decaying gas, exploding with all that———showering on all of us. *Alles kaput,* as the Germans would say. *Humpty-Dumpty sat on the wall with an overblown carcass ready to fall.* What a thought! One could laugh with tears in one's eyes!

The respite was over, and again we went on our way to "push" the Germans back into Germany. The next stop was another farm house for the night—thank God at least it was above ground. As we entered the farm house, we found ourselves going in to a sort of barn, or storage area. On both sides against the wall were mounds of sugar beets, of various sizes, from perhaps nine to twelve inches in diameter. We were told to accommodate ourselves among the beets. How would *you* like to stretch out on a mattress of sugar beets, of various sizes, and one for your pillow? *C'est la guerre,* Kilroy.

For some reason or another, I was called upon to see the captain with his officers in the kitchen with the farmer and his wife. The captain asked me if I could convey their request for a room with beds. Why me? I did my best with a bit of Yiddish expressed with a more definitive German accent, at which I was not too good and with a bit of English mixed in. The farmer and his wife got it, and said they would do their best to accommodate them. I suggested to the captain that some coffee packets and sugar would be most welcome. The captain thanked me.

I went back to the mounds of sugar beets, and leaning up against them—I had to squeeze among the fellows, I took out a K-ration with cheese and crackers and munched away, a swig of water from the canteen; and then finished, lit up a cigarette. I found myself reading with half-closed eyes on the verge of sleep. I put out my cigarette and fell promptly to sleep, embracing a large beet in my arms.

A book of verses underneath the bough
A jug of wine, a loaf of bread—and thou.
Beside me singing in the wilderness.
Ah, wilderness were paradise now.
—Verse from *The Rubaiyat of Omar Khayyam* (Fitzgerald)

The next morning out on the road again, checking the farm houses of the villages to our right and left. In one farm house I remember several of us on entering into the kitchen, the women and two young girls were taken completely by surprise. There was that dairy smell that permeated the room and part of the others. We assured the women that we were checking

War's end. Railway transport to Le Havre, France, port of embarkation to the U.S. The "40 x 8's": a designation given to the box cars by the French, during WWI—transporting "40 men and 8 horses" to the front lines.

Transport on the "40 x 8's"—waiting.

Refugees from East Germany fleeing the Russians.

Refugees from East Germany fleeing the Russians.

Refugees from East Germany fleeing the Russians.

Refugees waiting for transport.

Destruction caused by Allied bombing.

Destruction caused by Allied bombing.

Destruction caused by Allied bombing.

Stop for chow.

Refugees waiting for transport.

Rest stop—I am standing—my buddies seated behind the wooden rail:
Fresh air and sightseeing.

Setting out to meet the Russians.

Dressed to meet the Russians.

American and Russian officers.

My Platoon Sergeant Witt with Russians.

Altogether—I mugged my way to the front.

Another gathering.

91

I pose with the Russians.

Visiting Brussels.

Visiting Brussels.

Visiting Brussels—two buddies on my right. They did not make it in the end.

Brussels with a Jewish buddy. He was gone after the Roer River crossing.

Garbage and filth piled up outside our hotel.

Our hotel—Londres et New York.

Place de la Concorde.

Chow line—war's end.

Chow line—war's end.

My buddies and I.

Rest and relaxation—war's end.

A walk in Cologne.

German women—off-limits lecture.

Held in reserve—on my right my
Jewish buddy who did not make it.

ASTP—Spanish group, at Spanish Museum, East Harlem, NY.

I am posing on board ship sailing home.

On board—sailing home—any seat.

On board—any seat you can find!

Welcome home!

The last one has to be explained: AS (Air Shaft) We were going up a hill in Stolberg under fire. We went down to the basement of the houses, and found we could go up the hill through archways from one basement to another. A Signal Corps photographer asked for a volunteer. I volunteered. He told me to take a pose shooting at a German in one of the airshafts between two buildings. That was that. When we got to the States, I noticed this photograph on a billboard. I took it off, pocketed it, and I could see the back. It was written "An American soldier taking a bead on a German."

around. We looked through the bedrooms and living room on the ground level, and then climbed up to the attic. The ceiling walls were slanted on the sides in a V-shape, gabled. It was quite stuffy and warm, with an apple aroma. The floor was covered with a large quantity of small green apples, that were drying to a wrinkle, and turning brownish. We were tempted to try eating one, but thought the better of it. It was sunny when we entered, and then when it began to get cloudy, we left. You can never tell about the weather in Holland. One minute the sun would shine, and then in a few minutes, those big, puffy black and white clouds would come scurrying across the sky, bringing drizzle, rain, and showers. Then, in a moment, it could clear up. The raincoat was forever handy, folded over our belt, flapping in the back.

We walked along the road on both sides in single file. There was the smell of wood burning in the air. The chimneys of the farmhouses off in the distance emitted smoke. The smell was not unpleasant, it was almost aromatic. The ambience of such peace and pleasantness that permeated the surroundings, almost idyllic, gave an impression of another world, but only for a moment.

It started to drizzle again, and became quite chilly and damp. We seemed to be climbing some elevated areas as night approached. Then we descended into a flat area and came into view of a large bonfire with British troops warming themselves around it. There were Canadians, whom we came to relieve. A couple of Canadians approached and greeted us with tongue-in-cheek, and pointed to our posts, and wished us good luck. They chuckled as they moved on. Two more characters of our group, suddenly broke out with one of those stupid remarks; they couldn't take all this crap and mumbled on that they were not going to be killed for those damned Jews. They turned and hurried away, never to be seen again. Whatever happened to those guys?

I looked down on my post and couldn't believe what I saw. Some Canadians had burrowed holes the length of a man, into the side of the mound. I got down on my knees and looked in. Sure enough, there was a cylinder-like shape hole about three feet in diameter, extending inward about six-and-one-half feet. The hell with it! I was going in! I was so darn sleepy, I didn't care if the cave fell in on me. I burrowed in, rifle and knapsack ahead as a pillow. My nose was about six inches from the ceiling, which dripped at regular intervals on my pottee helmet, and promptly fell asleep, The Elixir of Good Health. The next morning I was awakened. I wiggled out of my accommodations, washed, of sorts, and whatever; had a hot breakfast, and off we went along the road to God knows where. We were never told. We were not to reason why, but to do and die.

The Germans were retreating rapidly, I suspected, into Germany. Some more deviations were made for checking small villages on the way. As night fell, the drizzle and cold air returned. It was, I thought, about mid-November, wintertime in Europe. We stopped in the middle of nowhere, and told to dig in. I was given the honor of going out to a position in front of the group. I decided not to dig in. I had my raincoat on. I just laid down on my back on the icy, watery, glazed earth, my knapsack as pillow to hold my head above my body.

In the distance, I noticed flames, in yellow and red, ablaze against the dark sky. There were troops of soldiers moving across in a straight line, silhouettes, almost like dark shadows of spirits from some *unterwelt*. As I kept staring at that horrendous conflagration of a village, my mind tended to invert my sight perception to a point that I began to imagine those shadowy figures were coming on to my position. If this was not enough, the cold wetness of the ice below me which was seeping through my trousers, started my muscles to tremble, shiver, and shake, raising my legs above the ground as if in a fit. On top of all this, my buttocks (ass, in the vernacular) was bouncing up and down, high-hoing as if I was on a horse, riding bareback. I was sure that if any of the fellows were to come by and look at me, their one comment would be, "You know, I think this guy is all jerked up."

This was as much as I could take. My usual comment issued forth, "To hell with it!" I got up and shakily strolled back to the group nestled in their foxholes, and slid into one with nary a word. The three of them looked at me and moved over with nary a word.

But then, they looked at me again as if waiting for some comment. So, I told them exactly what had happened out there on the icy ground. Besides, I just didn't like what was happening out yonder in the burning village with all those soldiers scurrying about. That said, they nodded, and moved again to make room for me to settle in. I leaned against the side of the hole, and promptly fell asleep, as sorts, actually dozed off in fits and starts. However, this being Holland, the water was slowly seeping there from the bottom of the hole. By morning as we awoke, the water had risen almost up to our knees. If only we would get out of this damn country!

Out again on the road, we moved forward, and eventually ran into the cook's outdoor service for a hot meal. We were served scrambled egg (powdered eggs), pork sausages, beans, bread and hot black coffee. This was surely welcomed. All we could eat. The hot coffee helped to drive the chills from our bones. After that interlude, we continued on. We didn't realize at that time that this would be the last day in Holland.

Toward evening, we stopped at on open field, and told to dig in. I took it upon myself, for some ridiculous notion, to go around, telling the guys to keep a cover over their foxhole. We had gotten a new infusion of Repot Depots. A couple of them popped up, and exclaimed, "Who the hell was that guy telling us to put a roof over our foxholes!"

Of course, I had no stripes, just a PFC making like a Staff Sergeant. I may have been out of order, but I thought I would give them the benefit of my experience. With that unwelcomed reception, I decided on a hasty retreat. Never again!

I was greeted by two young sergeants, completely new to me. I had the impression that they were ASTP men, newly arrived, with no combat experience. Without much ado, I was told I was now a runner, attached to the lieutenant, also newly arrived, and apparently a friend of theirs.

"What's a runner?"

I was told that I am attached to the lieutenant's command. That is more or less an *aide-de-camp.* I found out in time that that was somewhat of a Figaro, maintaining contact, communication, acting as a guide, and assisting in delivering supplies, food, and mail, between the company c.p. and the platoon when out in the field for specific operations and orders.

I was somewhat disgruntled at first for being so off-handedly treated like some nondescript, but I came to realize that this job had its virtues. For one thing, I was attached to the lieutenant—Ferguson, a competent, well-educated person, with whom I got along very well, who very rarely ended up in a foxhole. I came to enjoy whatever privileges and other considerations commonly granted officers. As our relationship unfolded, and with our common educational experience, we shared confidences on equal terms. I was glad to serve under him.

As for the two sergeants who dismissed me with such calloused disdain that I added their names to my list of those that would not be missed. They were both staff sergeants, both of whom needed names. I don't remember their last names. The one, who appointed me to the exalted position of Runner; the Big Shot, I named Gunster Knocker, and the other one, who maneuvered his way into a job at the Company C.P., he is, of course, *Harder Nusskoph.* He was later wounded by mortar shell-fire as he rested outside the C.P.

So, this was the last night in Holland. We were glad to get out of the foxholes when we were notified that there were trucks waiting nearby for us to mount. We did. They were one-and-a-half ton troop carriers with benches on either side, six men on each. There was no overhead cover. It was still pitch black, cloudy, and it began to drizzle, dank and cold, as usual. We had on our raincoats. We joined a long convoy of trucks, heading, as told, toward and into Germany.

On the way into Germany, we saw the first of the horrendous scenes of destruction which became so common as we traveled further inland. I was seated on the right side of the truck, overlooking the heads of the fellows seated on the left side. As we drove along the paved highway at high speed, there ahead of us, we noticed the sky was lit up by an inferno of yellow, orange, and red flames, reaching up far into the dark bleakness of night. As we approached the flames, we noticed the sign on the road pointing to the city of Aachen. Aachen was burning, almost completely. We found out later that allied troops had fought house to house to push the Germans out. Aachen was a key hub.

As we were looking over the heads of the row of soldiers seated on the left side, we noticed a scene as eerie as one could hardly imagine. There in the drizzly, lit up darkness, was the ghostly façade of the remains of a bombed out apartment building, with its opened framed space where windows once were installed. The flames reached up beyond the open spaces of the building façade. They appeared to dance a macabre ballet of shimmery figures in yellow, orange and red.

Below the façade, on a pathway, we noticed three figures, that I imagined to be women, in long coats and dark hats, slanted to one side of the head, dragging a level, flat, four wheeled cart, so common in Germany. Somehow, I had the impression, by the way their bodies moved forward, slightly bent against the drizzle and wind, that they were dragging a quarter section of a carcass that I imagined to be horsemeat. Two of them were in front with a makeshift harness around their shoulders and bodies and rope attached to the cart, alongside of which one other figure was bent over, and moving with both hands on the carcass to keep it from sliding off. They were moving on a narrow path that appeared to be on the outskirts of the burning city. *How Art the Mighty Fallen!* (*King Saul*)

We drove into the empty city of Stolberg (more likely the outskirts), which became somewhat of a rest and reconstruction camp. We were placed in reserve, for the time being. We settled in the empty buildings, and made ourselves at home, out of the foxholes.

Hot meals were resumed. A laundry unit was set up, where we lined up for showers, and were issued a set of newly laundered clothing from top to bottom. New combat shoes were also issued to those who needed them. Moments of relaxation; letter writing, and sleeping. Refreshed for the next push. A new group of Repot Depots joined our ranks to reconstruct our company. There were only a few left of our original company.

It wasn't long before we were alerted for the next push. For a few days, rain and overcast kept us in a hold position. When the sun finally came out, American bombers came roaring overhead and all hell broke loose . . . a tremendous, continuing roar of cataclysmic proportions. It seemed as if the earth was tearing apart. With that, our artillery was also adding their two cents. The objective was to take the high ground and clear the town of the Germans.

When all was ready in the late evening, we came out of our houses, and there before us was one of the steepest—I thought a good fifty degree incline—hill that had to be ascended. The air was charged with tenseness. Company A was to spearhead the assault. Three tanks were lined up with a squad of men from the first platoon placed on top of each one. The rest of the company lined up on the sidewalks in single file, I among them, along-side the buildings. When the order came through to ascend, we all moved cautiously.

Suddenly, all hell broke loose on our heads. In spite of the bombings and artillery shells we had showered on the Germans for hours, they were still able to respond defensively. We were greeted with a shower of eighty-eight shells from the screaming meemies as well as mortar shells. The shells were bouncing and exploding off the tanks, which stopped moving.

The men on the sidewalks ducked into the buildings. The men on the tanks took the beating. Most of them became casualties. I won't describe that scene. As they tried to get off, some took a direct hit, others were hit by shell fragments. There were those, I learned, who had made it to the top of the hill, off the sidewalks, and had taken refuge in the buildings there. They then came under heavy counterattacks, but managed to hold on.

Half a league, half a league
Half a league onward,
All in the Valley of Death
Rode the six hundred.
'Forward the light brigade,
Charge for the guns!' he said:
Into the Valley of Death
Rode the six hundred.

'Forward the light brigade!'
Was there a man damaged?
Not a soldier knew,
Some had blundered!
Theirs not to make reply
Theirs not to reason why,
Theirs but to do and die.
  —"The Charge of the Light Brigade," Lord Tennyson (Courtesy of *Story Poems: An Anthology of Narrative Verse*, © 1957 Washington Square Press)

Everything stopped. We were pulled back. A new assessment had to be made. Before I left the building I found refuge in, I was curious enough to examine books which were strewn about. I came across one which made my hair stand up. It was written in German, of course, and contained graphic pictures showing large, grossly fat, *vermin* (rats, in the vernacular) scurrying, helter-skelter, about the kitchen, eating everything in sight, and leaving a disordered room of garbage and droppings on the floors. The bodies were realistically depicted, but the faces were of sinister-looking Jews with long, ugly noses. I could only make out a few words in the text, but it left me with a sickening nausea. I wonder if these books are still in circulation.

We were beaten back, but we had to hold whatever we had gained. The men at the top of the hill had to be supplied with provisions and ammunition. I and two other runners from the second and third platoons were set up in a kind of halfway house between the Company CP and the men on the top of the hill, on the left side of the street. All requirements and other necessities requested were dropped off at our station, and we had the duty to get them to the top.

At first, we managed to skirt up the street on the left sidewalk when things quieted down, in the dark of the night. But there were times when we had to make a run in daylight, which placed us at risk of being spotted by the Germans, who immediately responded with gunfire and mortars. It must be said that the tanks were completely disabled in the street, and remained in place for two days. The mangled bodies of soldiers were still lying in the street, and could not be moved until the dark of night.

As we managed to settle in, one of the runners brought back a carton of food, labeled *TEN IN ONE,* a veritable feast, packaged for supposedly ten men. We were never served these repasts. The Headquarter Company personnel had that privilege. We opened the carton and found a large can of fully cooked, whole chicken, white bread baked round with a hard topping, a large can of jam, cans of pudding, beans, green vegetables, mixed fruit cocktail, applesauce, tea bags, coffee packets, whatever utensils needed, and a can opener.

We opened the cans, cut the bread, and laid the food on dishes we took out of the china closet, after wiping them with dishcloths laying about. The only water we had was from our canteens. There was no way of making hot drinks. Considering the circumstances, we gorged ourselves without restraint. There was no thought of saving anything, except, perhaps, the coffee, tea, and sugar. With each course eaten, out flew the plates through the open windows to the back yard. Then, our royal repast finished, we sat back and lit up cigarettes. Ah! Life could be really enjoyable, given half a chance. But that was not to be!

A messenger came up from the Company C.P. and deposited a batch of letters to be delivered to the group on top of the hill. It was my turn to go. I decided to go up through the back yards that extended about fifteen feet away from the houses, to form a kind of ledge that overhung a steep slope, leading down into a ravine filled with leafless trees. As I started out, I was suddenly seized with nausea and cramps. Of all things to happen right then and there.

It didn't take long. I must have been spotted by the Germans somewhere on the top of the hill. *Where in the hell were they anyway?* I heard the familiar keplop of a mortar going off accompanied by a swell of machine gunfire as it swept overhead into the trees. I took off on the run. But the body couldn't hold its grip on the innards, which burst forth with intestinal effusions as it sympathetically responded to each explosion of a mortar shell burst, which fortunately landed in the ravine. Each effusion was stimulated forthwith by a loud burst of wind—I could describe it otherwise, but I prefer to observe the delicacies, which propelled me onward with immeasurable speed.

When I got to the group, I deposited the mail and took off without a word. I started back with the fastest run I could attain—I outdid Forrest Gump, I'm sure. When I arrived at the station, I ran through the house to the incomprehensible amazement of the other two runners, saying I was sick as all hell. I ran through the doorway onto the street, turned right, and headed straight down to Battalion Medics. With a breathless huff and a puff, I explained my indelicate plight, which tickled their sense of humor and laughter. It wasn't funny, fellows. I was given something resembling Kaopectate®, which I drank for life's sake. I stood (I didn't dare sit down), and kept drinking for all it was worth. It was having its effect.

The medics took me to the laundry and shower mobile unit, where they explained my predicament to the officer in charge. I was told to strip completely and to enter the makeshift shower room. The cold shower revived my spirits. I soaked myself down thoroughly several times, not only to cleanse my body but also the memory of what had overtaken me. When I was finished, I was given towels to wipe myself, and a blanket to cover myself as I sat off on a side bench, to recoup my composure. My discarded clothing was taken to the backyard and burned.

When I felt composed, I was given a new set of laundered, well-worn, clothing from top to bottom, except for the shoes. I strolled back to my station in the middle of the street, steady like. The two runners greeted me with a chuckle. It never got to them. On the table were the half empty cans of food taken from the ten-in-one carton. I could not look at all this without a feeling of nausea. I told the fellows that I felt sick and needed to lie down. I told them to call me in two hours. I went up to the first floor where I found a cot on which I promptly slumped, shoes and all, and off to sleep.

I was awakened about two hours later. It was already getting dark. I felt much better. An hour into the evening, I began to feel well enough for something to eat. I managed to have a slice of bread with some jam. I made some tea, GI procedure, as I did back in Holland. The fighting up on the top started up, once again. The sounds of the bursting shells and gunfire were quite audible.

About ten o'clock, we had visitors from the top. Two of the soldiers, who were supporting one of their comrades, his arms wrapped around their shoulders, walked into the living room of our station. The middle soldier was hallucinating and trembling uncontrollably. No doubt he had had a psycho-traumatic breakdown, euphemistically called battle fatigue. He had the DTs, and had to be held down by both of his friends, after he was placed against the wall. One of the runners ran down to the medics for assistance.

His friends were trying to comfort him by repeating that he was among his buddies, and that there was no fighting outside. But unfortunately, the street outside was being cleared of the casualties, and of the disabled tanks which were being pulled way down the street by other operating tanks. The clanking noises of the tanks set him off.

"No! No! No! The tanks are coming! The tanks are coming! They're going to crush me! No, no, no! I have to get out of here! Help me! Help me!" His body was twitching, trembling, shaking. We had difficulty in holding his arms and legs down.

His friends responded. "Jimmy, Jimmy, they are our tanks. They have come to save us." This was repeated several times. The demented soldier just kept sounding off hysterically. There was nothing much else to do but to continue to hold him down. The three of them were remnants of those who were part of the original company from Camp Carson. Slowly, but surely, they were fading away.

It was not long before the medics arrived with a medical officer and a stretcher. The doctor gave Jimmy a shot of some sedative, probably morphine, which quieted him down. The four corpsmen put him on the stretcher, tied him down, and off they went.

This event shook the three of us all up. An attack by tanks, which I thought I was to experience later on, is one of the most frightening experiences any soldier could have. The sight of these gigantic dinosaurs . . . metal monsters, if you will, coming straight for you, spewing forth a steady stream of machine gun fire with that tremendous cannon aiming to blow you apart, especially if you are stuck in a foxhole, meaning to crush you like a tomato, or, yes, mangle you, or grind you into hamburger meat, bones and all, is not a pleasant thought. I could understand and sympathize with Jimmy's breakdown. They must have been catching hell up on top!

After the medics left, we tried to compose ourselves. We lit up cigarettes and settled down on the floor with our backs to the wall. We then fell asleep. The hell with it!

In the morning, we were called back to the C.P. Another push was brewing. Allied planes swooped down over us in a steady stream, hundreds of planes of all types. They laid down a barrage of bombs on the top, and on the city itself for about three hours. This time we meant business. The town had to be taken. The Germans did retreat, but left several elements to counter-attack to hold up the Allied Advance. We learned later that the Germans were forced to give up their defensive positions in the city, and move further eastward into new defensive lines.

When the bombing stopped, we moved up the same street on the sidewalk, alongside of the buildings, on either side. The tanks moved up in the gutter without troops on top of them. (We learned our lesson.) Halfway up, we heard the familiar *keplop* of mortars going off. We knew the shells were aimed at us. This time we ducked down to the basement of the buildings, where we found archways that connected the buildings. Terrific! We walked through them as we ascended the street with perfect cover. As we continued, a signal corpsman walked into our group, camera in hand—they were the official photographers—and asked for a volunteer. We all stared at him. Who in the infantry volunteers for anything? Nobody answered. But I, not following my good wife's admonitions did, with my usual expression, "What the hell!"

"What's to do" I asked him.

"I just want you to go into that airshaft between the two buildings. That reminded me of the railroad flats I lived in back in Brooklyn when I was young.

The airshaft ground was piled up with broken pieces of wood, glass, crockery, rags, newspapers, a veritable garbage dump.

"I want you to lie down in position on your stomach as if you were firing at a German," he requested.

So I got down on my stomach, put the rifle on my right shoulder, pointed it to the wall, and positioned my face and cheek against the stock of the gun, right eye on the range finder, tasking aim at the wall. The photographer took two shots, I didn't, and responded, "OK, that's it. Thank you very much."

I got up, wiped the refuse off my clothing, and headed for the rest of the group, which had moved ahead.

This is a kind of footnote. When the war ended in Germany, the 104th returned to the States and settled in Fort Dix, New Jersey. One day, as I was passing through the hallway on my way to the game room at the U.S.O., I noticed the bulletin board on the wall. As I approached it, I was surprised to see the photograph of myself aiming my gun in that airshaft. I looked around to see if anyone was coming, and without any compunction, detached the thumbtack from the photograph, grabbed it, and put it immediately in my pocket. When I entered the game room, I went over to a corner, took out the photo (it was a good shot) and turned it over to read what was on the back. It read, printed in red ink, "An American Soldier taking a bead on a German. *My God! What imagination,* I thought. But, I didn't mind. At least I was photographed in combat, and am recorded in the military archives of the U.S. Government. *"I was there, Charlie, taking a bead on a German!"*

Finally, I reached the group at the top of the street. We knew this because there were no longer any archways to go through. Instead, we found a stairway that took us up to the ground floor of the house. On looking around, we realized that this must have been a townhouse of a very affluent

German family. It was a corner house, with many rooms, baths, and some very attractive lighting fixtures. The house was empty of furniture, with bare walls and shelving.

I went up one flight to the bedroom, empty and bare as the ones downstairs. A couple of the guys were banging on the walls with the butt of their rifles. I looked at a soldier alongside of me and asked, "What the hell are those two guys doing?"

The reply came forth, "They're looking for wall safes!"

"Wall safes!" I exclaimed. "Do they think that the Germans would have left any money or jewelry in their wall safes, having cleared out every bit of worthwhile possessions from the house?" Incredible!

We descended the stairs and moved out to the main street to our right. As we walked along the street deserted of its inhabitants, we came upon an old, broken down jewelry shop, fully occupied by American soldiers rummaging through the store. The outside glass window was completely shattered. The soldiers were pulling out all the drawers from the large cabinets, hoping, I imagined, to find watches or jewelry. No luck, just spare parts to watches. I turned around, and walked out.

On my left, there was this big monster of a tank clanking its way down the street. On top of this tank above the turret stood this imposing figure of the tank commander, observing the scene, and giving commands to the men on the inside. Around the turret, there hung a bar stool and two small area rugs. I imagined that some time in their youth, they were members of the Boy Scout troop, whose motto was, "Always be prepared." Suddenly, the tank stopped. Two soldiers sprang out of the open exit of the tank, holding two empty, woven fiber bags, normally used for the flood control barriers, and jumped to the sidewalk. They ran into the shop, shoved the men aside, you don't argue with a tank man, grabbed the drawers, and emptied the contents into the two sacks. When filled to their satisfaction, they ran back to the tank, handed the building sacks to the commander, and hopped aboard. The tank took off, and so did we all.

We moved cautiously forward along the streets, and onto the open highway toward Eschweiler. From the highway, patrols were formed with a tank as leader. A squad of men were put on the thank and off we went, deviating from the highway to a village in sight. As we entered the village on the run, the inhabitants, elderly women and elderly men, dressed in their WWI uniforms, smiling with their one or two remaining front teeth, and waving white pillowcases and torn sheets, hollering at the top of their lungs, *"Alles kaput! Alles kaput!"*

The tank stopped, and off we jumped, and headed for the storage building and homes to search for any lingering German soldiers. We did find two Hitler Jungen, kids of twelve or thirteen years of age in uniform, hiding behind some crates in the storage building. They surrendered willingly, no problem there. This procedure was followed as we walked along the highway.

Here I quote from the *Training and Combat Record of the First Battalion, 415 Rgt., 104 Division* to give some orientation of the area in Germany where we were fighting.

"Our unit was not confronted with German counterattack fire. The companies edged up to the town of Eschweiler. Patrols felt out the situation. the 329th Engineer cleaned out hastily laid minefields fully left by the retreating enemy, and prepared the way for its penetration. On November 22nd, the battalion cautiously entered the town. Within a few hours the industrial center was cleaned and completely taken."

The next day was Thanksgiving Day, and we were resting comfortably in reserve. The troops had much to be thankful for, that goes for me, too. Other units of the division stormed Weisweiler, took Frenz, Lamersdorf, Inden, and crossed the Inde River. Abel Company, mine, went into positions near the lake and an empty viaduct, and contacted the ninth division on its right flank. Baker and Charlie prepared to jump off to the Roer River from Luchenberg. Our company settled in for a rest and reconstruction.

Our meals improved, hot and full. The weather was getting very cold, and I and several others went out exploring through the attached sheds of other buildings next to ours. We came on a bonanza of pressed coal bars, made from coal dust of the mines. We carried a whole batch of these over to the living room of our house. Other fellows ran out and got their own supply. We distributed a batch of coal bars to other occupants of the house in adjoining rooms. We made improved stoves from very large empty cans lying about. And so we warmed up the house to our comfort (better than lying in frozen foxholes).

We were now in the first days of December. Other units were being poised to move toward the Roer River, a proper area for starting the next move to Cologne, after crossing the river. However, our company was deplete of men and material, so we were kept in Reserve. With thoughts of the coming of Christmas, C.P. loosened up in giving some of the men (remaining) who have been through the campaigns from Holland on—passes for rest, good food, and catching up with rest and correspondence—general relaxation in whatever way.

About mid-December, the good First Sergeant Ginelli called a few of us into his office, and said that he was giving each of us a six-day pass to Verniers, France, a U.S.O. Rest Camp, close to the German border. We were told to have our packed duffel bag, helmet and rifle ready at 0900 the next day. A truck will be waiting for us.

The next morning, after breakfast, we assembled at the Company C.P. where a one-and-one-half ton covered troop carrier truck was standing. We boarded the truck, duffel bag and all. We seated ourselves on the slats on either side, five each side. There were ten of us. We were all smiles, going on holiday with the blessings of Uncle Sam free of charge. We greeted those we knew, and said hello those we didn't know.

Traffic was heavy on the main road to France. We had frequent stops to relieve ourselves, and resorted to our K-rations for lunch.

It took several hours before we reached Verniers, and when we arrived at the USO, we checked in. We were taken to rooms, four men to each one. It was late afternoon. There was still time before supper.

We were told to report to the supply room where we were to receive a set of new clothing—the works, and then to the shower rooms after we put our new clothes in our room. We had hot showers, a welcome relief, with plenty of soap, which we slapped on repeatedly to get that feeling of the muck and mire off our faces, arms, and bodies. That done, we shaved and began to feel and look like human beings. Then to a hot supper of many choices, dessert and coffee. After a good smoke, off to bed, and a long, pleasant sleep—a deep sigh of contentment and relief.

The next morning, Greenfield, Svenson and I had an early hot breakfast together. After, we looked at each other with blank expressions. What to do? Sitting around for the next four days could be very boring. On leaving the mess hall, we noticed a map of France and Belgium on the wall. We looked at each other, pointed our index fingers to Brussels (Bruxelles) through Liege. Why not hitchhike to Brussels, it shouldn't be too difficult as the distance didn't seem impossible. It was decided, pass or no pass.

Before leaving the building, I gathered up by 620 Box Camera, a couple of K-rations, a canteen of water, and stuffed them into a GI shoulder bag, which was used to hold our gas mask. We left the mask behind. Down to the street we went, and off to the highway heading west. We checked for the sign to Liege, and proceeded to the highway.

We walked along with our thumbs pointing in the direction of Liege, in hope of getting a lift. Finally, a GI truck stopped for us. Fortunately, it was heading for Liege, where we got off (thank you very much), and walked along the river about a mile. Then a British lorry stopped for us, heading for Brussels. The two Brits invited us to join them. We hopped in the back, and off we went on to Brussels. They were really nice chaps. We chatted with them a bit, and asked them if they knew where the USA U.S.O. was. They said yes. When we got to Brussels, they stopped at a crossing, and pointed the way a few blocks up the street. We bid them a thankful farewell with a gift of some American cigarettes, which were highly appreciated. Off we went.

When we arrived at the U.S.O. in the late afternoon, we checked in, registered our name and outfit—no questions asked. We got our keys to a room on the first floor, three cots, and flopped on them, and off to sleep. We got up in time to have supper. We gathered up plates and utensils, placed them on a tray, and as we passed along the serving table, each course was dished out by GI cooks, as was customary, bread, dessert, and black coffee. Couldn't have it any better.

Then to our seats around a table. When finished, off we went to visit the main street of the city. On the way down, we came across the local cinema, which was playing *A Yank at Oxford,* with Robert Taylor. That was good enough for us. We got our tickets, and entered. The theater was hardly filled, so we took loge seats, and enjoyed the show.

It was late evening when we left the cinema. Down the street we went, following the sound of music as it drifted upward. When we got to the source, we came upon a hotel bar, lights ablaze, filled with soldiers, representing all the outfits of the Allied forces. The music came from some kind of juke box. Some soldiers were at the bar, arms around the waists of the local angels of the night, boozing it up, laughing, talking, giggling, chuckling, with a hail-well-met slap on the back. Perfect sympathetic gestures toward each other—Whites, Blacks, Hindus, Americans, Canadians, French, Polish, British, and what have you. Perfect comradeship—good to see and feel, all's well. The Germans were finished! You know. We went downstairs to the rest room.

We stopped at the urinals, unbuttoned our flies, took out our phalli, and as they functioned, we chit-chatted on the raucous scene which was taking place upstairs. About halfway through, out of the corner of my right eye, I noticed that I was being approached by an elderly, gray-haired woman with a cleaning brush in her right hand, and a pail with cleaning

116

fluid in the left. Then she started to nudge my right arm, vigorously, to get me to move away.

Ce n'est pas fini!! Ce n'est pas fini!" I protested.

It didn't do any good. She wouldn't give up. The hell with her. I had to finish. I wasn't going to be intimidated, even if it meant ending with black and blue abrasions. Finally, I finished. I shook off the few drops that remained—I was told to do that at CCNY by the physical training instructor when I started the sessions.

We buttoned up and stepped aside to watch the matron approach the stalls, which were fully occupied. Three of them. She started to bang on the doors. The occupants let out a stream of invectives and protests not appropriate to reveal. They didn't faze the old lady. She just kept on, and we were laughing all the way up the stairs to the street. We went back to our quarters, and off to sleep.

The next morning, after breakfast, we decided to take in the town. It was not very interesting. The streets were quiet, dirty, and drab. The weather was cloudy and drizzling. Typical for December. We decided to leave the next day, but first for the celebration at the hotel bar in the evening. In the morning after breakfast, we decided to leave after lunch. I wanted to take some photos with my trusty box camera. We walked about again and found the stores still shut, and the drabness of the town and weather still remained. We had a group photo taken with my camera by a soldier passerby.

After lunch, we set out on the highway to get a lift to Liege, and then to Verniers. When we got there, it was already dark. We found the place all astir—a hustle and bustle. The sergeant greeted us with, "Where the hell have you guys been?"

"Well, Sarge, you know we were in town," I said with a wink.

"Well, get your gear and report down in the street. There are trucks waiting to take you back to your outfit."

"What's happening?" we asked.

"The Germans have broken through our lines, and are moving through Belgium," he replied. We didn't know it then, but this was the Battle of the Bulge.

When we got down to the street, we found trucks, motors idling, lined up, perhaps eight or nine of them. The sergeant asked us for the name of our outfit. "The 104th Division," we said. He took us to one of the trucks and told us to get on board. We recognized the fellows that came with us from Eschweiler. When all the trucks were filled, they took off in a line.

They moved cautiously. We had no idea in which direction the line was moving. No headlights on, we moved in perfect darkness, except for some lightness from a partial moon. The sky was clear. The stars were shining. We were silent in the truck.

As we moved along, we stopped several times only when we heard the buzzing of a plane swooping down at us. We jumped off and ran into any house along the road, the occupants of which viewed us in astonishment. Nothing was said. Nothing happened. The plane would take off. Back again on the trucks. We sat . . . hardly relaxed, and our minds wondered and wondered what the hell was this all about.

In Brussels, we found the bars ablaze with glee and optimism as if it was just about over. "Wars's End and Victory." Now we found ourselves fighting for our lives. Hitler and his generals were uncanny. Our generals and G-2 were caught off-balance. Somewhere there was a miscalculation. This will cost lives.

We then came to a crossroad. For some reason, our truck deviated away from the main line of trucks, and headed on to another road by ourselves. The trucks stopped for a moment, and we heard the sergeant and the corporal companion discussing the route to be taken. They evidently had a map which they checked, and then we hard them mention the destination to be Eschweiler, from whence we originally came. So we proceeded.

It didn't take long before we began to hear the buzzing of a plane overhead. Probably the same damn plane that was buzzing us all along. We had no idea whether it was a German or Allied plane. As soon as it seemed to be coming down on us, the truck stopped. "Everybody off!" came the command.

We all jumped, one by one. As I came down on the roadway, my pottee helmet came off my head, and banged down on the cement. The noise was so loud, one could hear it all the way to Berlin. But of all things, the truck had stopped in the middle of an overpass, stretching over a main highway below. Where to go?

I ran along the roadway a few yards away from the truck in case it would be hit and explode. I ran up to a post and got through the two metal railings that extended from it. I moved over to the post, put my arms around it, and crouched down on bended knee. What else. The plane came *schwooshing* down with a tremendous roar, with a wind of hurricane force, enough to blow one out of his shoes. But it did not fire into the truck. It then ascended straight up, turned around, and came in on us for another pass. It did not fire. Was the pilot kidding, having a good laugh, or just decided to ignore us?

Whatever, he took off not to be seen or heard of again. I returned to the overpass roadway, took a last look at the highway below; my palpitating heart in my throat, picked up my pottee helmet, and mounted the back of the truck with the others. We all sighed with relief. We lit up cigarettes, and settled back. The truck eventually reached Eschweiler. When we were brought to our outfit, things were astir. We were issued overcoats and galoshes to bear up under a miserable cold snap of about twenty degrees below. There was some snow on the ground which glazed in sheets of thin ice. We had no idea of what was going on, only that we were moved from village to village over sheets of ice, slopping to the crackle of breaking ice.

There was a heavy dark overcast as if one could feel the coming end of the world. God and the Germans were pouring it on. We could only imagine that somewhere, our troops were catching hellfire, frostbite, and death. *"C'est la guerre, mon ami!"* The infantry soldier bears the brunt of hell and damnation!

Finally, we stopped in some village, and found quarters in abandoned houses. Our platoon (or what was left) took over one house. I and a few others decided to scan the sheds around us, searching for those elusive pressed coal briquettes. We found one pile, and loaded up with as many as we could carry.

There was a stove in the kitchen next to our room. We loaded it with briquettes, got it fired, and before long, the places were warm and comfortable. We each took turns at sentry duty outside the house, with two hour stretches. When my turn came, I stood out there in the dark at minus twenty degrees, and ended up with the worst sinus cold imaginable. I had so much phlegm, I could hardly breathe. When I was relieved, all I could do was to drink hot tea as often as I could. I eventually managed to overcome this, and I realized that I was tougher than I thought.

Here, I must quote again a passage from the *Combat Record* of the First Battalion, 415 Rgt., 104th Div.

While the Western bank of the river was being flushed, the Germans launched their powerful counter-offensive into Belgium. The Battalion built strong defensive positions in Merken and the vicinity, to guard against any eventuality. Frequent contact and combat patrols were sent out. While the enemy threw men and materials in an all out last effort in Belgium, Christmas and the New Year came to the Redmen (*my outfit*), with its turkey and packages from home. The festival spirit was not lacking, and the men considered themselves lucky. (*Nonsense!* I don't remember getting anything. I was doing my best to keep from freezing to death.) On January 9, the battalion went back to Weisweiler into division reserve, set itself up comfortably in town, and began a training schedule. The German bulge was shrinking, and the Russians were making great progress on the road to Berlin. Things were looking better and better all the time. But there was still the River to cross.

I could only imagine that the above was produced by English majors, ensconced in the warmth and protective study of the Regiment Headquarters, who never had the pleasure of standing guard in minus twenty degree temperature in the open, or nesting in a foxhole in snow in ditto temperature, benumbed in feet, nose, and fingers. When reading the exposition of such fertile imaginings, I am filled with great pride for having stood up to it all!

It must be mentioned that these euphoric images of our progress were written by hyped up, probably former ASTP men who never spent one day in combat. Our outfit was in Germany when the Germans invaded Belgium on their way (hopefully) to Antwerp. In other words, the Battle of the Bulge was going on below us. We didn't know it at the time. We never saw or had any turkey, or Christmas goodies or packages from home. For us it was only a dark, overcast, miserable, frost-ridden existence. So much for the Battle of the Bulge and Christmas. But, for all that, we did consider ourselves lucky when the facts came out.

We were kept in reserve for a few weeks in January, at the end of which we were moved to a town along the Roer River. We would be staged for the next big push to take Cologne, on the Rhine River. This was to be a major and bloody undertaking. The preparation was to be intense. The *Record* mentioned the towns of Haven and Echtz. I never did keep track of the towns and villages we spent time in, we moved about so often. Whatever the town, these were experiences, unusual as they were, worthy to be mentioned.

For one thing, the town was fairly large. Company A was stretched out for some distance along the shore of the Roer River. Part of the first platoon was quartered in the center of town, to which I was attached. Another part of the platoon was quartered at the edge of town, along the river, from which they would send out patrols. It was part of my job as runner to bring up mail, packages, and provisions to that group. I had several guys to help me. When we had packages and provisions to carry, I procured some cord or belts to secure them to ourselves. At other times when there was only mail, I took it myself.

When we were set to go with our shoulder packs, we took the road to the left of town, and walked about one-quarter-of-a mile. The road then turned left, making a right angle, and then continued on for another one-quarter-of-a mile to their station. But it wasn't that easy. We had *the* walk at least once a day.

In time, somehow, the Germans across the river espied our daily excursions, took range and started to plop mortar shells on us as we walked. The keplop of the mortar firing was becoming very familiar to us, so that when we heard them, we just took off. Fortunately, at the turn of the road, there was a remnant of a stone hut—probably a smokehouse for bacon. It was roofless, and showed only four walls standing. We did find some security within these walls. When the firing stopped, we slipped out, turned left down the road, which to our good fortune, had trees on both sides, until we reached our destination. This was a daily occurrence. We did manage this without any casualties. Returning to base was without incident. We ran most of the way back.

There were times when I had to go it alone. One day as I was looking through the door window of the house along the road, I was overcome with an underlying fit of anxiety at the thought of walking along the road on an errand of delivering mail to the outpost. I had a most peculiar premonition that I would be leaving myself exposed to sniper fire. I decided the best thing to do would be to cross the road and slip down the slope to the adjourning field of trees.

So, when I was given a batch of mail to deliver to the fellows over yonder, I walked across the road, slipped down the slope on my heels, and turned left. Being about five-feet six inches, I just managed to get my head below the road, except, perhaps, for the slight appearance of my pottee helmet slightly above about one inch. I didn't know that, though. I walked along cautiously as the slant of the slope and the uneven ground below my shoes made going somewhat difficult.

I got about fifteen feet along, when suddenly I heard the crackle of gunfire from across the river, and the whiz of a bullet zinging slightly above my helmet. I slouched down, and took off. Needless to say, my heart was pounding, my body all tensed up. I made fast track with my Pottee helmet rock and rolling on my head. I never did get a proper fit. *Those bastards!* I exclaimed to myself over and over again. It really amazed me to think that I should have had that premonition. This was the first time the Germans had used gunfire from across the river. I was lucky to be alive. I continued this practice several times, but I was never shot at again.

Things did ease up somewhat. Allied planes began to appear above us each day, and were showering the other side of the river with bombs. This probably accounted for the let up of the mortar and gunfire from across the river. We were more relaxed in carrying our supplies and mail to the outpost.

One day, I came across a large drum filled with hard lumps of brown wax. Ah! If I melted down some pieces and filled a few cans or glasses with the melted wax and added a cord wick, we could have some light in our rooms for reading or card playing. Large pots were easily available in the kitchens. I filled a couple of these pots with pieces of wax which I prepared with my bayonet. I found a large metal garbage pail and laid in pieces of wood which I found lying around. I got a fire going, and managed to lay the pot of wax over the can to melt the wax. I scoured around the open ground, filled with small stones, broken glass, and small pieces of string cord. I picked up string, which I thought would suit the purpose.

I then proceeded to reach for small empty cans, like the C-ration type, which I found lying about. I picked up about ten of them. I found a long stick to which I suspended ten-inch pieces of string stretched along the stick from both ends. I decided to work on the kitchen table. I then went through the other rooms and found a few shelves filled with books. I took enough books to give me two piles to the height of seven inches, one pile on either end of the stick, which I laid across. Under each string, I placed an empty can, which I did my best to clean with some rags found in the kitchen. I then poured the melted wax into each can.

When the pouring was finished, I waited until the wax had hardened. It did not take long, considering how cold it was outside. That done, I cut the strings with a kitchen knife I found in one of the drawers, allowing about one inch of wick above the wax. I tried one which I intended to keep for myself, and after about five minutes, the wick continued to burn. Success! This was it! I handed out the remaining nine cans to the fellows in the house, and everybody thought I was a 10 percent do-it-yourself American. At night, at least, we lit up the rooms for reading—some fellows had paperbacks, card playing, letter writing, and talking.

Then there was a very unusual incident. Instead of going to the outpost by way of the road, I felt confident enough after all that bombing to walk diagonally across the open field directly. Another item of security, in a way, were the number of tall, cone-shaped haystacks that littered the field. As I walked along, I tried to keep myself covered by those haystacks, which were quite broad, and placed at regular intervals. They seemed to be so placed that they covered, inadvertently, the intervening spaces between them. I felt quite covered.

Each day, I went forth with my errands without incident. But one day, I was shocked beyond belief. When I returned to the C.P., I saw three tall German paratroopers, the winged insignias were on the jumpsuits, standing there being interrogated by a battalion officer interpreter. I asked one of the fellows what was this all about. He said these paratroopers just walked into the C.P. and gave themselves up.

"Where did they come from?" I asked.

"They were hiding in haystacks out on the field," he replied.

"Hiding in the haystacks!" I exclaimed, "I've passed those haystacks a half-dozen times in the past few days. Holy Moses! They could have slit my throat!!"

I thought they were meek enough. They would have gained nothing by that. However, if I had spied them as I walked across the field, and brought them in, I would have been a hero, probably a Silver Star one. Boy, what a story I could have manufactured! But this was idle thinking. I was alive and that's all that mattered.

Then there was another incident. One night I had to deliver some packages, which I could manage myself, to the outpost. When I left the C.P., I told the sentries that I would be back shortly. On returning I would call ahead, "I'm coming in fellows, coming in." I never bothered with passwords. The fellows knew me, and were used to my goings and comings.

When I got to the C.P., I was called in by the captain who told me that Teebles had been shot by one of our men, who were in the foxholes along the river. He told me to take Svenson, and to bring in the body. I suggested to Svenson that we take a chair with us. Carrying a slumping, dead weight of a body could be very awkward. I did not know about the men who were detailed to maintain surveillance in foxholes that were dug in along the river and around the perimeter of the C.P. They were always extremely nervous.

We picked up one of the kitchen chairs and walked down toward the river. On the way, we called out to the fellows to let them know we were coming, and also to ask them if they knew where Teebles' body was lying. We were told where to find it, which was in a field between the foxholes.

We couldn't understand how he got there, but we could easily surmise that he had left to relieve himself, got lost on the way back, and wandered into the sight of a very nervous Repot Depot.

We hoisted Teebles' body on the chair in sitting position, and we each grabbed one side, lifted it, and walked straight to the C.P., careful not to step into a foxhole. We were glad that those nervous characters in their holes didn't take potshots at us. As we walked to the C.P., I recalled Teebles back in Camp Carson. He was low in I.Q., from Appalachia, and was more or less protected by others who came, probably, from the same area. Most of his friends were now gone. I remember that back in Camp Carson we were buddied up on the rifle range.

As I took aim to fire the target that was raised and lowered by a team of men entrenched about one hundred feet in front of us, Teebles would tap me on my shoulder to indicate that the target was coming up. When it stopped, I would fire, say, five rounds. The target was then lowered, the score was taken, and indicated on a white board that was raised, and of which he made a note. A new target was put on the frame and raised.

For some reason or another, the target was raised and lowered very erratically, which made it difficult to get a proper aim for firing. Teebles would explode in curses of the worst kind. He would start off saying, "Motherfucker this! Motherfucker that!" over and over again. This repetitive obscene allusion so offended my sensibilities that I stood up, pointed the butt of my rifle right before his face, and exclaimed, "If I hear you say those words again, I will cram this butt down your throat!" I was really enraged, haughtily so, I now confess. Teebles looked at me with blank astonishment, without saying a word. Needless to say, nothing more was said. I had very little to do with him after that. Now, I was carrying his dead body, and if I were able to communicate to him, I would express my apologies for my behavior back in the camp. That expression was so often used among all classes of soldiers that I came to accept it as part of the human reaction to the slings and arrows of outrageous misfortune. When we returned to the C.P., we deposited his body for the medics to arrive with a stretcher to take it away. Svenson and I sat down along the wall as well, lit up cigarettes, looked at each other, and up at the ceiling, and blew out our smoke in restful relief. *C'est la guerre, mon ami.*

As the days passed, with allied planes flying daily over to drop bombs on the other side of Roer, we were lined up before the battalion medics for cursory physical exams, which included the ubiquitous short arm inspection, and then next door for dental examination. This has to be mentioned to establish the battalion medical station for what was to occur tragically later.

Things were quiet for a while, except for the mortar firing that was taking place outside our buildings by the engineers. They had come across a case of German mortar shells piled up at the rear of our building together with the mortar gun. The engineering officer and his men were enjoying themselves plopping mortar shells over the river to the annoyance of the Germans.

One sunny day, when I returned from one of my errands across the field, I was told that one of the fellows had set up a barber shop—hair cutting at the magnificent sum of one dollar, on the third floor of our building. I felt I needed to have my hair trimmed. I felt I should look proper if I ever "got up there!" So, I ascended to the third floor, without expecting the tragic occurrence that would befall us.

The barber, who was very tall, had set up a chair on top of an empty wooden crate, near, but not too near, the window to catch the light. There was a fellow in the chair and two others seated on chairs along the wall that stretched away from the window. I and two other fellows sat on chairs along the opposite wall that extended from the exit, but not facing the window. As usual, we were just making small talk about our experiences, whatever. The Allied planes were flying overhead, as usual every afternoon, crossing the Roer River, and unloading their bombs on the German side.

Suddenly, inexplicably, the planes turned around from the German side, and opened fire with their machine guns right at our building and all the other buildings as well. A wave of bullets came through the top window narrowly missing the barber and his client! We all went for the floor, but when the planes started to unload their bombs on our camp, we went for the exit. The noise of the explosions rent the air outside our building. Fortunately, none of us were hit, yet. We ran through the exit doorway, down the steps, two at a time, helter-skelter. Men were coming out of the side rooms. Down to the second floor landing, without tripping. The first floor landing was a different story. Someone must have tripped. As we came down two or three steps at a time, some tripped on top of the pile on the first floor landing. Down at the bottom of the pile of bodies, legs, arms, and voices were crying "Get off my friggin' back! Get off my friggin' back!" and so on. I was flying down two steps at a time, managing to avoid the pile up, keeping to the banister on the right. Fortunately, I was the last man, and so had no one to trip over me.

I managed to get to the room on the right, stepping lightly (sorry, buddy!) over the pile, and entered into a three ring circus. There were three fully bedded cots, one against each of the three walls in the square room—one to the left, one up front, and one to the right. The space under each cot was fully occupied with squeezed bodies of very much alive soldiers. One of them had his left arm exposed, with the palm of his left hand scarcely clenched, his left thumb prominently extending out.

Then men were running around the room in a panic as the bombs outside continued to explode like chickens whose heads were chopped off. As they got to the exposed thumb, they inadvertently stomped on it one after the other. The poor soldier was yelling in agony, "Stop stepping on my thumb! Stop stepping on my thumb! You so-and-so-and-so," with an explosion of cuss words that outdid the very essence of the use of "motherfucker," which seemed rather tame in comparison. In a few moments, his left thumb took on the proportions of a small knockwurst. Too bad! But in the end, he would report it to the medics and probably end up with a Purple Heart medal and a 10 percent service-connected disability with the V.A. I decided to slump down with my back to the wall between two cots, and seated, smoking nonchalantly a cigarette. What the hell! If the bomb comes down on us, there is nothing much else to do but pray.

"So, let us pray!"

The bombing stopped as suddenly as it came. The planes drifted off, and all was quiet again, an eerie silence except for the yelling that arose in the streets. We all unscrambled ourselves, moved down to the ground floor, and out through the doorway. In the street, fellows were running to the battalion C.P., yelling to beat the band. When we got there, Holy Moses! The battalion medical building was a shambles, dust and smoke rising overhead. The planes had gotten direct hits in spite of the Medical Red Cross on the roof. It seemed that the bombardiers were using this insignia for target practice. Those stupid, incompetent bastards! They scored two doctors, two dentists, three corpsmen—dead. There were other casualties, some minor, some more severe. That was that, *monsieur!* Friendly fire! With such friends, who needs enemies. As the saying goes.

Needless to say, we were all shook up. It took several days to calm down. Fortunately, the cookhouse was not touched. So we survived.

For the time being, we would be without a medical station. Efforts were made to replace our Medical Facility with new personnel as soon as possible. Things settled down again as new Repot Depots joined us, including a few non-coms in order to bring the division up to full strength.

We were being set for the big push, the one that would bring an end to German resistance. We hoped.

We received a new Platoon Sergeant named Witt. We came to like him as a humane, considerate, leader. He was of medium height, but burly. He was built like a bear, with strength and machismo to match. He had no hangups on race, religion, politics, or any ideological, half-baked, mushy-minded moral imperatives to change the world in which happiness, goodness, peace, and brotherhood, not to mention sisterhood, would reign forever, and ever, and ever to eternity.

He joined us one night in our assembled room lit up by the flickering lights from the candles I had made. In the glow of the candlelight that resembled the atmosphere and light of a Rembrandt painting, he related one of the oddest stories of his life in answer to our curious inquiries.

He related how he was inducted into the engineer corps, and participated in the various invasions and campaigns of North Africa, Sicily, Italy, and through Northern Italy. He won his sergeant stripes, shipped to England to await the invasion of France. Training exercises were observed during the day, and in the evenings, he spent at the local pub (he was from Texas), frequented by members of the Allied forces. British soldiers were the more numerous. With beer, music of sorts, and female frequenters of all sorts, it all made for a rollicking good time.

Well, he took a shine to a beautiful well-stacked British maiden who responded in kind. Somehow, he thought she would be more than usually permissive to his charms and swan song. But this was not to be. It seemed that this fair maiden had a British boyfriend also stuck on her buxom charms, and who had no intention of sharing her with anyone.

Inevitably, like in all good westerns, the boyfriend confronted Sergeant Witt, with not only a verbal invitation to get lost, he proceeded to apply some meaning to his exhortations, with a powerful blow to the sergeant's face, very much to the Britisher's misfortune. Sergeant Witt, born and bred in Texas, the land of Remember the Alamo, being no slouch, reacted with all the brawn of his powerful frame and arms and in true John Wayne fashion, beat the you know what out of this poor, forlorn lover, who was soon immobilized against the bar. This inauspicious confrontation started a true uproaring, helzapoppin brawl, worthy of any western movie, in the pub, among the American and British soldiers. The MPs responded with full force of their riot equipment, and finally restored peace and loving quiet. Sergeant Witt was led off to the U.S. Military Tribunal, charged with disorderly conduct and assault. He was stripped of his sergeant's rating, and sentenced to three months in the military jail.

But as fate would have it, he was offered a way out. A week before D-Day, he was offered an unusual proposition. Men were needed to defuse the sea mines along the landing shores of France before the troops would invade the beaches. If he accepted, his sergeant rating would be restored, and his record of the sentence would be expunged. He grabbed at the opportunity. Better than nothing, rotting in jail. The rest was history. Sergeant Witt did not relate how it was all done. Only that he was involved in clearing the shoreline of mines. He was not involved in the actual landings. He was returned to the destroyer that brought the engineers. Later, after the troops landed, and fought toward Germany, he played his part as a member of the engineer corps.

As his outfit moved up through Germany to the 104th Division, he was transferred to our Company as the need for platoon sergeants became critical. So he came to us much to our benefit, for he proved to be a son-of-a-gun leader and a fearless rifleman. It was pleasure to see him pursuing Germans as if he was on a hunting trip going after wild boars.

It wasn't long before things began to stir. Long boats were brought up and laid along the riverbank. More Repot Depots were constantly being brought up to fill the company ranks. None of these appeared to have had any combat experience. The men who had held positions along the riverbank were called in for the assault across the Roer River. This was to be the main assault to break Hitler's resistance. It was in the month of February, still cold, damp, and nasty. An army chaplain appeared and it was announced over the loudspeaker that prayer service would be held outdoors. Insofar as it was non-sectarian, I joined in the power of prayer, which I fully acknowledged, was very comforting, and in a group. It served to establish a common bond.

As the Battalion Combat Record would have it, "When the battalion moved into the jumping off place at Hoven and Editz, the Roer was steadily rising. To the south the Germans had blown a dam to flood the river so as to stop the Allied surge toward the Rhine. American Engineers repaired the damage. The water reached its high point and then began to recede. The flooding of the river held off the all-out drive for Cologne for a few days, but it permitted the pilots of the P-47s to bomb and strafe, and the forward artillery officers (Allied) to divert fire on enemy strong positions."

What this record did not mention was the overflowing of the banks of the river into the trenches that we were to find on the other side.

For two days, we sat in our rooms fully packed and ready to go. In the evenings, by candlelight, we thought of home, mostly, of our loved ones, of the moments when we were together, enjoying each other's company of love, of the outings, of the travel we indulged in together. We all thought as we spoke, that if we came out of this in one piece, life will never be the same. A few fellows spoke their somber thoughts: "This is going to be it for me. I have a feeling that I am not going to make it." I never had any such premonition. Not that that assured my survival, but as it turned out, they did not make it. I have always wondered that those who had those premonitions were victims of a repressed will to survive.

For two days, the bombing from the air on to the other side not only trembled the land there, but it had the same effect on our side. What a beating they must be taking!

Just before push off, we were served a hot meal of the usual—pork chops, beans, mashed potatoes (desiccated), string beans, applesauce, and bread. Most of us who had been through these assaults before, ate every bit of it. Who knew when the next hot meal would be, if we survived.

A-Day, 23 February, finally came. At 2:30 A, B, and C Companies with support elements of D pushed across the river with the aid of the engineers.

We moved down to the river where the assault boats were placed. There would be two squads of eight men each, one on each side of the boat. We pushed the boat into the river and hopped in. As I had walked down to the rear, I was handed a reel of telephone wire, which felt like a ten pound weight. In the boat, I laid the wire alongside of me, my rifle was slung over my back on top of my knapsack, and grabbed one of the hand paddles as ordered. There were boats on either side of us, one on our left, and one on our right.

My thoughts were interrupted by a called for break in our travel to Paris. The going was very slow with frequent jerky stops. Finally, we got a much welcomed respite. The truck moved off the road on the right in patches of grass, bushes, and trees. We went about relieving ourselves, and stood around or moved about to stretch our legs. We had a one-half hour break for a luncheon snack of K-rations. When the time was up, we hopped back on the truck, and took off.

Talking on the truck had diminished, and most of the fellows leaned back for a catnap. Myself, I wanted very much to continue my story in memory.

Yes, yes, where was I. Oh! The assault. This really turned out to be the big one. Our survival and futures were at stake.

VII

The Assault

The sergeant was in the back as Helmsman. "Faster! Faster!" he called, "Faster! Faster!"

The river wound downstream, ever so rapidly. We had to contend not only with the distance of about seventy feet, but also against the current that was dragging us downhill, which tended to slow us down.

If that was not enough, when we got to about the middle of the river, the Germans who seemed to have survived the bombing, suddenly opened up on us with machine gunfire, spraying the bullets at an 180-degree arc. Fortunately, we were not touched, but the boat on our left took a tremendous spray that riddled their boat and men with bullets, which incapacitated the boat, and caused it to drift down the river. We could hear the men calling for the medics. I found out later that Greenfield and Svenson were in that boat. I never saw them again.

Our boat hit the shore with an uncontrolled lurch, that threw us forward. "Everybody out! Everybody out!" came the call. I was about to meet muck and mire. I grabbed the reel of wire, moved forward to the front of the boat, and brought my legs overboard in a pile of mire. As I tried to climb over the muddy slop of muck, I kept slipping, dragged down by the stupid reel of wire. Finally, I made it, with the help of my knees. When I got to the tip, I leaned over a trench and went down, belly-whopping, headfirst, with arms extended in front, the reel of wire accelerating my pitch down, where I met mire again at the bottom. Fortunately, my extended arms kept my face from slapping into the mud.

I righted myself by turning onto my back and in a sitting position. I did my best to wipe mire off my jacket. It was pitch black. I suddenly became aware of a body alongside my right. It was a tall, heavy-set body of a German soldier on his knees, whose face was slammed into the side of the trench, muck. It (he was quite dead, you know—so now he is an it) had a heavy, gray overcoat on, no helmet, showing a head that was balding. Hitler must have been scraping the bottom of the barrel with middle-aged men, over fifty.

I got to my feet to hurry on, and as I passed over the protruding feet, I exclaimed, "Sorry, Buddy, I have to pass you by." You see, I tried to observe the amenities. As long as it was a *dead* German, it was my buddy. As I moved along, slipping in the mire, I met another body, exactly positioned as the first, quite dead, you know. "Sorry, Buddy, I have to pass you by."

Then, the unexpected happened. I was seized with violent cramps—for duty to be done. I had two possible choices. Either continue on, let it all come out, and end up with the seat of my pants full of it. This was hardly a choice. I certainly could not manage to function, and besides, it would be humiliating to be found such, if I were wounded or even dead.

No! The only thing to do would be to set down, and relieve myself in spite of the machine gun fire overhead, and the mortar shells bursting somewhere up front. On the side of the trench above, I set down my rifle, the reel, my army belt, and the knapsack. I took out a wad of toilet tissue, which I always carried, from my jacket pocket, raised up the bottom of my jacket, lowered my trousers, and set to. Ah! A joy! I then proceeded to open the fly in the front to complete the exorcism. I wiped myself as best I could, and dressed myself properly.

That whole procedure completed, I buckled up my trousers. I shouldered my knapsack, grabbed my rifle, and placed it in my left hand, and that ridiculous reel in my right hand. I schlepped forward in the slippery mire, slowly;

So that was it—Combat!

A combat infantryman's credo:

The muck and mire,
The shittin' and pissin'
The shleppin' and shloppin'
Der schiesen und bombin',
Oy vey iz mir!
Gott in Himmel!
Alles kaput!

Fortunately, I think I was the last man in line moving forward, most of them having passed me by in their haste to catch up with the others. I could hardly move in haste with that reel of wire that I felt was increasing in weight steadily, and eventually up to about fifty pounds. That's what it felt like. The only good thing about that was it caused me to crouch very low as I walked along the trench. Bullets were ricochetting overhead on the ground on my right. I began to hear the *keplot* of mortar fire ahead of me, and the explosions on my left. I came to a left turn in the trench. There ahead of me it was all happening.

I made the turn and moved forward, warily. The ground was dry and sandy. Daybreak came with the rising sun. Then there came a stop. For some reason or other, the group were lying upright on both sides of the trench, hoping against hope that no shells would drop on them. The Germans were up to their usual tricks; lay you down with the machine gun fire, and then let you have it with mortar shells.

I set myself down on my knees, face and body against the left trench wall. I unhinged my shovel which hung from my knapsack on my back, and started to dig into the soft, sandy trench wall. I reasoned to place my face into the hole. With helmet on my head, my pack on my back, I thought I had sufficient protection from any zinging shrapnel from mortar shell explosions. I could settle for shrapnel cuts to thighs, legs, arms, and ass, to give me a fifty-fifty chance of survival. However, there would be no chance of survival if a shell plopped right down behind me. I would be shattered. What a thought!

So far, so good. I was among the last in line of the group. Hell was breaking loose, say, about thirty feet ahead of me. After about an hour or so, the shelling and gunfire stopped. Evidently, other outfits on both the right and left of us had successfully confronted the Germans, and also to mention the Allied airplanes were flying overhead, constantly unloading their bombs on them. The Germans were focused to retreat.

Soon our line began to move forward sporadically. Then came the sad sights. Men on both sides of the trench, wounded, shattered, moaning, calling for the medics, and a few dead. No time to take count. Lots of them. The saddest sight of all was when I came across Lieutenant Ferguson, the best I could ever ask for, lying against the wall of a half circle shell hole blown into the trench, fortunately only wounded in his right thigh. Sergeant Knocker was lying dead beside him.

I hailed the lieutenant, put my reel of wire down, and saluted him, which he returned with a smile. I wished him a full recovery. I never saw him again. He did recover well, and I was pleased to be told by Sergeant Ginelli, a few weeks later, that the lieutenant had commended me for holding onto that reel of wire. I was the only one to do so. There were three oth-

133

ers who were given the reels to hold on to, but I was the only one that came through with mine.

Finally, by about noontime, we reached the end of the trench, which ramped up. When we got up the ramp, we were told to move to the C.P., which had been set up in one of the houses of the village. When I walked into the C.P., Captain Fox, seeing that I had the reel of wire, ordered a sergeant to gather up a few men, and with me, to string wire from the C.P. to about five foxholes that were established around the C.P. semi-circle, a short distance away. We were now in Reserve.

We relayed phones to each foxhole to be wired for communication to the C.P. The Sgt., two men and I strung the wire, moving back and forth from C.P. to each hole. The month being February, a short month, it was dusk before we finished, about fifteen hours since we prepared to cross the river—no sleep, hardly anything to eat or drink. Back in the C.P.—no hot meal, just K-rations, which I opened after slumping down against the wall. The can had cheese and bacon, which I chewed away with bits of hard tack. Halfway through, my head started to droop, and I fell into a deep snooze.

I was suddenly awakened into consciousness by a sergeant with the words, "Wake up, Soldier, the foxholes are reporting Germans in front of them."

I could barely get up. My muscles were stiff and painful. I grabbed my helmet and gun, and exited the C.P. There were about ten of us assembled in the pitch black darkness. We started out, and moved along a foot path alongside the field on which the foxholes had been dug on our left.

We stopped and were told to scale about a five-foot slope leading up to the top. As I tried to scale the slope, surfaced with a massive quantity of pebbles and small stones, my stiff, uncooperative legs kept sliding down. No matter how often I tried to climb up, the result was the same, slipping and at times falling to my knees.

Suddenly, I felt a gun being jammed painfully into my kidneys. I turned to see a short, asshole of a lieutenant (a bar insignia on the front of his helmet), and with these threatening words, "If you don't get up this slope, I'm going to blast you to kingdom come!"

I stared at him. *That son of a bitch pulled a gun on me! That son of a bitch pulled a gun on me!* I exclaimed to myself. He was lucky that I was not one of those southern hillbillies. He wouldn't be long for this world.

The lieutenant was truly a stupid asshole. A little ass he is. Ah! A Burrito! Lieutenant Burrito! Didn't it occur to him that I had a rifle, and could find some occasion in the dark under combat conditions, to accidentally blow *him* to kingdom come? But fortunately for him, I was not the type. We had Lieutenant Schlimazel back in Camp Carson, who also threatened to use his gun on those he thought were trying to hold back on their duty. He ended up with a nervous breakdown. When we went into combat, he developed the insight of how easily he could be done in by the men he threatened. There is more to say about leaders up in combat, but that is a subject for another time. I did the best I could, and managed to get to the top. I slipped a few times, but to hell with him, let him do what he wants.

The only thing I could not figure out was, where the hell did he come from? I never saw him in my outfit. Was he some damn repot depot, or some jackass of a sergeant that got a field commission? Actually, it didn't matter. He turned out to be as much an officer as some of those other characters that were sent up to us. And that's not saying much. So for me, I was to be his runner, allied to a burrito; a little ass.

So much for that. Being as I thought he was, *El Burrito,* he lined us up across, side by side, and from the rear. A brave guy, you know. He ordered us to move forward, gun in hand. It was pitch black, you know, so I made sure to keep in line, and not to stray. I thought it best to place myself at one end as we walked ahead, making sure not to step into any of the foxholes. We called ahead to the men who were in them to make sure they wouldn't mistake us for Germans.

Ahead, there was an outline of a group of trees. It occurred to me, a much unpleasant thought, if there were Germans in the midst of those trees, they would open up a fusillade of machine gun fire that would mow us down like shafts of wheat. *Alles kaput!* If that would not be enough, the mortars would open up and drown us in a shower of whistling shells of explosives. "That would be a pretty mess!" Again, *alles kaput!* There, standing alone with pistol in hand—and being from Texas, as I found out later, a shout would arise, "Remember the Alamo!"

But nothing really happened like that. Something else did. One of our group, evidently being without thought, walked on ahead, and was soon lost in the darkness. Suddenly, a shot rang out from one of the foxholes to our left. A cry for the medics went up from someone in front of us. We ran over in his direction, shouting to those characters in the foxhole to cease firing, and found this young fellow in agony on the ground, a repot depot. El Burrito leaned over to ask where he was hit.

"In my left arm," he replied.

Fortunately, a lucky break. A million dollar wound, that everyone was praying for.

We helped him up to his feet, someone took his rifle, and Lieutenant El Burrito called the whole thing off. He had had enough. So did we. Someone grabbed the wounded man's right arm, and placed it around his neck. He then helped him down the slope, and walked him back to the C.P. We followed. There the medics were brought in. He was placed on a stretcher in a sitting position, and with the waving of his right arm, he smiling bid us all good luck and happy returns. We all smiled, wished him the same, and off he was taken to be shipped to that earthly nirvana, an English hospital. The lucky stiff.

The next morning, I was introduced to El Burrito as his runner. I had no idea if he recognized me as the one he threatened to blast away or not. No matter. I thought it the better part of good sense to let it pass, but not forgotten. No way could I gain any advantage by mentioning it to anyone. In time, I was to establish an uneasy relationship with him.

> I grew so rich that I was sent
> By a Pocket Borough to Parliament.
> I always voted at my Party Call
> And I never thought of thinking for myself at all.
> I thought so little, they rewarded me
> By making me the ruler of the Queen's Navee.
>
> —G&S *HMS Pinafore*—V

At daybreak, *"no, not breakfast;"* K-rations were the order of the day. We had to maintain contact with the Germans, who were retreating, helter-skelter, to get to the Rhine. We were not kept in reserve, in site of our losses. We moved along the road in line as the motor vehicles and tanks moved along in the center. Every now and then a group of about eight men was put on a tank, as we deviated along a side road, which led toward a small village. As we approached the village, the tank men hyped up the speed, and we Gung Ho-ed, Hi-Ho Silvered, and Ride him, Cowboy! straight into the village square, scaring the poor units of elderly men, bent with age, in worn World War I grey uniforms (home guard), waving white handkerchiefs.

Up on high, through open windows, elderly, grey-haired women were waving white pillow cases, shouting *"Alles kaput! Alles kaput!"* The tank stopped. We jumped off, and ran into the houses to check for German military stragglers, arms, etc. We came across three young Hitler "Jungen," in uniform, hiding among the straw of a warehouse shed. We ordered them outside, took their arms, and put them on the tank as we rode out of the village to form the main line.

So the day wore on as we dragged along, stopping only for short periods, when we could grab a bite of chocolate, fruit bar, hard tack, a can of anything we could find in our sack, or jacket pocket. The deviations into the villages off the side roads continued on our search missions.

Just before dusk, the battalion halted in a small village on the way. We billeted in any number of small, deserted houses, I and three others were assigned to bed down in a house at the exit of the village. No sentries to be posted. An announcement was made for a hot meal. At last! We grabbed our mess kits and cups, and ran back up the road near the Battalion C.P. where the cooks had set their hot food containers. As each of the cook's helpers sat behind the containers, they ladled out the portions of food as we passed in the chow line with our empty mess kits, cups and utensils.

Lo and behold! They served hot dogs, sauerkraut, mustard, beans, mashed potatoes, string beans, two slices of white bread, and hot coffee. Gourmet food!

The four of us took our kits back to our lodgings, made for the kitchen table, chairs, and sat down in ravenous mastication of this food fit for the proletariat. When we finished, we felt the need for some kind of dessert, which we thought of finding in these German rural homes. We decided to check the closet alongside the kitchen. We broke the lock, walked in, and found to our amazement shelves loaded with all kinds of vacuumed glass jars containing stewed fruit—pears, apples, peaches, cherries, and plums. We went for them, ravenously opening each of a kind. We flipped out the round wax disk, stuck our fingers in and pulled out a piece here, a piece there, as we filled our mouths and stomachs as fast as we could manage. When satisfied we had had enough, we went into the living room, and stretched out on the rug against walls, falling into a deep sleep.

But toward morning, I had a sickening dream. I dreamed that I was back on that liberty ship we crossed over. The weather was stormy and the ocean was in turmoil. The bow of this ship would be raised high above and let go to flop downward. Up, down! Up, down! Up, down! And with each upheaval, the ship would roll first to the left, and then to the right. With all this, I felt my stomach contents reacting in perfect sympathy. *Oy, vay iz mir!* I then ran to the rail of the ship because I knew it was all coming up.

With that, I awoke and headed for the doorway with fast, unmeasured speed. Around the house, and against the wall, it all heaved up. *Oy, vay iz mir! Oy, vay iz mir!* What a rotten taste!

"You did it again, Sancho! Will you never learn?"

A few more times. *Oy-y-y!*

Down the road the battalion was on the move again. El Burrito came along to check on us. He took one look at what was happening and said, "Go back to the battalion medics, and see if they can give you something."

Finally, I stopped retching, went back to the house, grabbed my equipment and rifle and walked back up the road. The men were moving alongside the road, and the vehicles were in the center moving slowly with them. I did not have to walk too far, but when I got to the spot where the medics had spent the night, there was nothing there except a few corpsmen, still packing to leave. I asked if a doctor was available, and was told that the medics had already left. Surprisingly enough, I was beginning to feel much better. My stomach had settled down, and the nausea had subsided. I took a swig of water from my canteen, and washed out my mouth. After which I drank a little.

Now to get back to my outfit. As I walked along the road, I hailed a passing jeep, and asked the driver for a lift to my outfit way down the road. I explained to him why I came to be there.

"Hop on!" he said, as he brought the jeep to a halt. I hopped on in the back where two soldiers were sitting. I imagined they were battalion C.P. personnel. I settled myself on the folded canvas hood above on the edge of the back seats with my two legs suspended between the two men.

As I sat there, I placed the butt of my rifle on my right thigh, gun nosed up. I had the sensation of riding shotgun on the old western stagecoach. I was beginning to feel good. My nausea had completely subsided. The sun was shining, and the cool air freshened me. I almost felt like a cockeyed optimist. The Germans were on the run it seemed, but only for a moment.

It was not long before the jeep caught up with my outfit. I hailed the guys from my outfit with a "Hiya, fellas!" with nary a wince in return. I asked the driver for a halt, which came, and I jumped off with a "Thank you, I appreciate that very much." He replied with his right arm raised above his head. I said goodbye to the two soldiers in the back. I found a place in the line on the right as it moved forward. El Burrito turned his head to see me back in line. But it was all too good to be true. We could see the outline of houses on the edge of some town or village as we were approaching.

Suddenly, in the distance ahead, we heard the boom of German artillery being fired. Then came the screaming meemies overhead—*Plow!* with a thunderous clap as they landed and exploded, fortunately not on top of us. We took off to the right, across an open field, *unfortunately.* I had the sense that the Germans were setting us up into another trap—force us out onto an open field, rake us with machine gun fire, and blast us to hell with mortar shell fire as we had experienced several times before.

A few years after the war, historians writing about the military tactics of the German generals pointed out that the greatest number of casualties among the Allied infantrymen came from mortar shell fire. Somehow, it seemed as if our top command had not learned the horror of this devastating practice.

We continued to move or run across the open field; in spite of the sweeping machine gun fire. As the mortar shells dropped and blew holes in the ground, they gave us some protective cover from the raking bullets. But, it was imperative that we move forward. As we all did, I ran from hole to hole in an advancing diagonal line from left to right, right to left, always crouching low, fortunately not being hit by zinging bits of shrapnel or bullets. Always as Colonel Blimp of World War I fame, looking for a better 'ole. As a youngster after World War I, when I came across cartoons of the Adventures of Colonel Blimp, always looking for a better 'ole, as he was drawn crouched down in a shell hole, and then shown looking out over the edge of the 'ole, for a better one to run to. I did not understand it then, but now I did.

Going from hole to hole, I became aware of a young repot depot following right behind me. Finally, after dropping into a hole, this youngster, probably about eighteen or nineteen (I was thirty then, an old-timer as it was figured), slid down behind me. I was getting a little annoyed at this, and exclaimed, "Are you following me?"

"Well," he replied, perfectly at ease, "I figure you have been through this many times before. If you survived so far, I guess you must know the ropes."

Well, he may have a point. I probably would do the same thing if I were in his shoes. But I was not flattered. I was only a PFC, and I wanted to remain so. To hell with achieving a higher rank! This was not a private, profit-making corporation, where being up there assured you of life, liberty, and pursuit of happiness!! In this corporation, you're lucky to come out alive.

I didn't want any responsibility in seeing to his welfare. He was not a child. So I answered, "OK, if that's how you feel, you're still on your own. I wish you luck!"

He nodded his head.

When the opportunity arose, I crawled out of the hole, and headed for one diagonally to the left. I came across one that seemed to have a sheet of corrugated metal on the top. I slipped through under the cover, headfirst, followed by the youngster, and came directly face to face with Sergeant Witt, of all people. Next to him was another soldier with a bloody gauze pad held over his right eye, groaning with pain.

"What happened to him?" I asked the sergeant.

He replied, "He was hit in the eye with a shell fragment." I gave him the gauze from my first aid kit.

My friend and I adjusted ourselves into a kneeling position. It was pretty close there and very uncomfortable.

Ten minutes later, El Burrito came by, moving on his haunches, and appeared in front of our hole. I could see him, gun in hand. "Come out, it isn't so bad now," he ordered.

But the sergeant replied, with all the diplomacy of a Wit(t), with such perspicacity, such sagacity! A sage of such profound discernment, worthy of a Voltaire: "With all due respect, Sir, *Ah've got no armor plate 'round mah ass!*"

The three of us in the hole were completely taken by surprise—astounded, you might say. Such undaunted chutzpah!

A worthy man after my own heart. A sergeant well worth looking up to. His expression was one for the book of quotations—a combat infantryman's credo: "Ah've got no armor plate 'round mah ass!" This mastery of a deeply felt expression should be emblazoned on the back of the jacket of every combat infantryman in yellow letters.

We all suppressed a chuckle. El Burrito moved off, but he returned about fifteen minutes later, and looked down at us, gun in a very shaky hand, shouting very harshly, "Come on out, *this is an order!*"

Well, I guess he really meant it this time, "Ass or no ass."

I crawled out, maneuvered myself forward, snakelike for a few paces, got to my knees, set myself up for a fifty-yard dash, as I learned when I was on the racing team in Junior High School, and when all seemed safe enough, I took off in the direction of the houses at the edge of the town. I was followed by the others. We got to the first house without incident, entered, and made for the cellar. Down we went.

Holy sassafras! A sight one never could have imagined. There on the left sat an American captain on a wooden crate, a lieutenant alongside, and behind a non-com with two privates. Right in front of the American group, about fifteen feet away, stood a tall Aryan, Teutonic appearing German officer, blond, blue-eyed, dressed in a long, grey coat, a smart officer's military hat on his head.

He was lecturing, uprightly, in perfect Oxford English, on the rationalization and justification of Hitler's and the German people's moral right and duty to save Western Civilization from Marxist Imperialism, international Jewish "attempts to corner the money of the world," and to conquer it as well. Also, it was the German peoples "duty" to conquer it as well. Also, it was the German people's "duty" to obliterate the degenerate permissiveness of the so-called free, treacherous societies of Europe. Only Hitler and the Nazi party has the vision of bringing order, peace, brotherhood (for Aryans only), heroic, correct thoughts that could only come from the imposition of Aryan purity of race, and Aryan moral principles. Besides, the real enemy of all mankind was that scheming Marxist country to the east—Russia, of course. The United States should have joined them in fighting Russia, instead of against Germany.

The captain was very patient, listening to this verbal claptrap. It was evident that the German officer was very serious, and it only demonstrated how supportive he was of Hitler's megalomania. The captain, whom I imagined was probably a professor, or instructor in European history or philosophy, proceeded, line by line, to dismantle the very underlying, half-baked, delusionary, hyped up premises of Hitler's ideological maze. After taking each piece of the maze apart, he showed that this central core of Hitler's self-cognitive beliefs was nothing less than a Caesarian attempt at power over the Western World; to loot the wealth, gold, possessions, objects of art, industries, mines, and other resources to run Germany's economy, and, as well, to rob and plunder the banks of Europe, and especially the wealth and possessions of the Jews, which has been the policy and practice of Christians since the creation of the New Testament.

That said, the captain got up, and with finality said, "That's enough nonsense. Take him the hell out of here!" The lieutenant and the non-com signaled the two privates to take the German officer in tow. The German officer was ordered to raise his arms, and to head for the exit. The captain faced us, as we all saluted him, which he returned, and we all joined him to exit the house.

We all walked to the center of town, where we caught up with the main force, moving toward the end, leaving the houses to be checked by Army units behind us. The German officer was turned over to battalion headquarters. We continued our way toward Cologne, not reaching it before one other major unforeseen incident.

VIII
Germany

As mentioned before, we continued our practice of deviating off the main road to check on small villages at a mile or two inward to the left or right. This time, as dusk began to fall, we stopped, and part of our company of about thirty five men were given orders to proceed off the main road to the right supported by a tank, which we did not mount as we walked toward a town to be a checked and quartered for the night.

We reached the town in darkness, and proceeded down the main street, followed by the tank. The stillness laid over us like a dark shroud. We sensed a kind of eerie foreboding that one experiences on entering a dark cave without end. We checked each house, mostly of three or four floors, on both sides of the street. When we reached the end, it turned to the right. For some reason, it was decided to call off further checking—a fatal mistake, and to take up quarters back up along the street. The houses were completely deserted. The tanks turned about and took up a stand at the beginning of the street off the main highway.

Men were then set up in various buildings along the street. I and three others (including Finkelstein, an ASTP man, a native of Chicago) were set up in the first building at the beginning of the street, near the tank.

We settled in and decided to make ourselves at home. We went through the hallway to the rear exit, out to the yard where we relieved ourselves, washed our hands with some water from our canteens, and wiped our hands with a bit of cloth, laying about. We sat down at the kitchen table, took out a K-ration of whatever taste, opened up the can with one of those makeshift cutters, provided, and proceeded to partake of our repast. We had to decide on maintaining sentry duty. We decided one man every two hours. Only one person had a watch, which had to do. We picked lots of helmet, 1-2-3-4. I picked number 1.

The repast finished, each fellow took a position next to a wall, sitting down, legs stretched out, with back against it, smoking a welcomed cigarette for relaxation before snoozing off, which, unfortunately, was not to be.

It didn't take long. We began to hear shouting and gunfire out in the street. We went to the doorway, looked to the right from whence came the hullabaloo. There in the middle of the street, about seven houses down, was a gigantic German troop carrier with a mounted eighty eight cannon. The Germans were firing at a building above, from which firing was returned from the windows. The rapid fire of the BAR (the Browning Automatic Rifle, handled by the soldier who didn't think he was going to make it), was very audible. The Germans were shouting, *Kommen sie heraus! Kommen sie heraus!* ("Come on out! Come on out!")

Nobody came out. The firing continued. Well, the Germans decided on a more drastic measure. They maneuvered the mouth of the cannon, pointing it straight at the building, and gave our heroic "Remember the Almo" progeny of Jim Bowie, Davy Crockett, and John Wayne a matter to consider. They decided, wisely, to *Kommen heraus,* with hands up.

For us, what to do? We looked at each other. This was a very grave matter. I suggested we go through the hallway to the rear exit into the backyard where we might find cover, or even be able to jump over the fence into the next yard. An eighty eight cannon was nothing to contend with. We could figure on an advancing regiment of our own division to come through this town, perhaps in the morning. That idea didn't seem to suit them. Finkelstein suggested we hide in the cellar. I wasn't happy with this, but I went along.

We went to the cellar door, opened it and looked down. We noticed three mattresses that the former occupants had thrown down the steps. We stepped over the mattresses on the way down, and noticed two open bins, one each against opposite walls. One bin was filled with potatoes, and the other was filled with coal briquettes. Well, the thing to do, we figured, was for two of us to stretch out on top of either bin, and to cover ourselves with a mattress. OK, agreed! First we took the remaining mattress, and laid it across the door, slide up. Finkelstein and I got on top of the potatoes and covered ourselves as best we could with a mattress. The other two, whose names I cannot recall, got on top of the coal bin against the opposite wall, somewhat located under the stairs, and covered themselves, also as best they could, with the other mattress. It was not as uncomfortable as it sounds. They had the added protection of the stairwell above them.

Then silence, with mounting apprehension. In no time, we heard the rumble of the oncoming German carrier, and the footsteps of the Germans outside as they approached our building. *"Kommen sie heraus! Kommen sie heraus!"* the cry went up. No reply. We could feel the heartbeat thumping away at an increasing rapid rate. I could feel my heartbeat moving up to my throat. The Germans then entered the house.

We could hear the raucous sound of their heavy boots clogging about. Unfortunately, it seemed as I thought of it, we had overlooked the remnants of our repast on the table. Well, it must have given us away. We next heard the creak of the cellar door being pushed open against the mattress. We heard one of them say, *"Amerikanishe soldaten schlafen in keller."*

"Kommen sie heraus! Kommen sie heraus!" came the order.

We didn't move. Then down the steps, it seemed like a round metal ball had been dropped, plop! plop! plop! as it bounded down each step. Then, plow! The explosion rent the air! The sound waves reverberated from wall to wall. Fortunately, it was a concussion grenade. No shrapnel.

That was enough! We jumped off the bins, put our backpacks, rifles, and belts under the mattresses, and shouted, *"Kamerade! Kamerade!"* We surrendered. We then proceeded up the steps. When we got to the doorway, we put our hands up. Two Germans, one on either side of each of us, grabbed our arms, and faced us to the exit of the house. I felt the gun muzzle being jammed into my back. We were pushed into the dark, cold street among the German soldiers.

Immediately, two other Germans took hold of us, and began to empty our pockets, checked our wrists for watches, opened our jackets to check the lining for pockets, examined the contents of our pants pockets, while muttering to themselves, *"nichts mit nichts."* Nothing with nothing.

It should be mentioned that when we were putting our gear under the mattress, we also emptied our pockets of valuables and placed them under, including that one wrist watch. It is difficult to explain this impulsive gesture that seemed to well up from an inner feeling that we would return to claim them.

They then prodded us to walk down the street toward the troop carrier. Sergeant Witt and others were still coming out of the houses on the right where most of the firing had taken place. Then, on the left side, the heavy weapons platoon filed out, hands up, leaving all of their equipment behind. Satisfied that all of us were out and now assembled, the Germans proceeded again to prod us down the street, shouting, *"Schnell machen! Schnell machen!"* (Faster, Faster!) I did my best. I kept asking myself the question, *What happened to the tank men?* Not a shot out of them. I could understand them not wanting to take on a German eighty eight, but still it was their duty to help the guys who were under attack. Anyway, they were not around. And where was El Burrito? This was not a pleasant situation for us. We had heard of American soldiers being shot at Malmedy in the Battle of the Bulge. What happens now?

We came to a cross street, and were turned to the right. The stillness was overbearing. The houses were abandoned. The air was cold with a nip. Those twinkling stars above were looking down at us with indifference—God's children! There was an eerie feeling in the air, as if the spirits of the former inhabitants were still there, watching us sullenly, as we were goaded down the middle of the street. Out in the distance, the next town was in flames. The silhouettes of American soldiers were walking along a road adjacent to the edge of the town. The Americans were advancing. As sure as hell, the town we were in was surrounded. The Germans had nowhere to go with a bunch of American prisoners.

We were stopped at a few houses from the corner, and were ushered down the basement of one of them. We settled in as best we could on wooden crates, or on the floor against the walls. I sat with Sergeant Witt on a wooden crate. We were watching closely the German Communications non-com with his headphones on, seated at a large console from which communication cords protruded. He pulled and plugged into several outlets in the board frantically, as it seemed, without result. When the German captain approached him, inquiring if contact was made with their command, the reply was negative. They seemed to be at a loss as to a solution of their problem. Here they were with a handful of American prisoners with nowhere to go . . . a puzzlement. From whatever I could understand of their conversations, I was able to conclude that they were in as bad a situation as we were.

I leaned over to Sergeant Witt, and in a whisper I asked him if he was having the same thoughts as I. He nodded.

I whispered, "It seems they have lost communication with their command. They must have been left behind to hold up our advance as much as possible, and now they seemed to have been abandoned. They're stuck, lost, surrounded, and unable to decide what to do. We're in an excellent position to try to convince them to surrender. (Some chutzpah!) It won't be long before the rest of our battalion show up. We were really only on patrol."

Sergeant Witt agreed, but suggested we hold for a while for their embarrassing situation to sink in. A few hours later, we were ordered out of the house into the street. The sun was already rising, and the daylight lifted our spirits. We were then walked ahead along the street in the direction of the next village, which was still raging with fire and smoldering with smoke. However, a few houses along, we stopped alongside an open field, surrounded by trees, on our left. We followed some German soldiers onto the field, and stretched out on the ground covered with patches of wet grass.

Something next happened that I could hardly imagine. A German soldier stretched out alongside of us and offered me a K-ration chocolate bar, probably one he picked up from the table in the house we left behind. It was an unlikely, generous, friendly gesture. Is it possible the German soldiers were beginning to sense their peculiar situation? I, of course, accepted the chocolate, and thanked him very much in as best a German sounding Yiddish I could muster (interspersed with English, which he seemed to grasp). As he seemed to be in the mood to converse with me, I elicited the following portions of his life.

He was in his forties, a machinist, with a wife and two children. He was drafted into service as all others in his outfit, and he was homesick. After fighting for over two years, he was tired of it all. He and his outfit were transferred from the Russian front, of which he was very happy, as were all the others. They had enough of the bitter, deadly cold frost and snow. The severe Russian winter was without mercy, and without end, for which they were ill-prepared. Hitler had surely abandoned them there. The transfer to the Western front was a reprieve. At least they were in home country, fighting Americans, a different people than the Russians, more like themselves. I got the impression that being taken prisoner by the Americans would be a welcome relief; a confession of a battered morale. This thinking was to our advantage.

After an hour or so of this, we were then ordered up, onto the street again, and then walked ahead almost to the edge of town. But, we stopped at the last house on the right, and ordered in where we settled down on whatever chairs, crates, boxes, or on the floor against the walls, for some comfort. What next? The big question! I sat down next to Sergeant Witt and told him of my conversation with the German soldier. He was now convinced that this was the time to start a campaign to turn the table around.

We decided that I would take half of the Germans near the door, and he would take the other half in the rear. The sergeant had no knowledge of German, but we did find a few Germans who understood English, in both halves. That also made my sales-pitch so much easier.

The idea was to convince them that the war was *kaput;* all over for them. They had nowhere to go, and no high command. One way or another, they would all end up as prisoners anyway, since a larger force of American soldiers was on the way. As prisoners, they would have all the food, safety, warmth, and rehabilitation of a rest camp. I described the one I observed from the road as we hiked along at Camp Carson. German prisoners in Bermuda shorts were playing basketball outdoors; a rest resort atmosphere. Certainly to be appreciated, rather than be taken prisoners by the Russians—God help them! None of the Germans shied away. Neither the captain nor his lieutenant, as well as the non-coms, made any threatening gestures for us to keep quiet from the outside as they looked in. They really looked troubled and at wit's end. Fortunately for us, there were no SS men in the outfit. The German Captain, for some reason, impressed me as an academic type.

Sergeant Witt, who had done his best with his group, came over to my side. We stepped to the doorway and looked out. The German Captain and his men were standing and talking to each other. They looked up at us, blankly. We responded very carefully and sympathetically with an expression that it's all about over, and they didn't stand a chance. There was no response. They just stared at us. Suddenly, attention was drawn to the left of us by sharp sounds of a movement of men. We saw a group of American soldiers turning the corner from whence we had come, led by an officer.

We looked at the German captain and said, "That's it, it's all over for you. Resistance would be suicide!" The captain agreed. He took out his pistol from the holster, and gave it to Sergeant Witt. The other officer did the same, as well, the non-coms handed over their guns. I acquired the captain's binoculars.

The captain told the non-coms to call in the men from their foxholes out in the field beyond the houses at the edge of town. We had no idea of their existence. The German G.I.s came running toward us with their hands up their heavy gray coats were caked with mud, their faces unshaven, their baggy trousers also caked with mud and grime. As they came toward us, they lowered their arms, and stretched out their hands to shake ours, and even to embrace, like long lost relatives. We backed up, of course. We appreciated the gesture. Better this way than a barrage of bullets. What a relief for all of us. *Alles kaput!*

For some reason, in my elation, I was seized with the impulse to run up to the American officer to tell him that the situation was well in hand. When I approached him, I saluted, and noticed that he was a colonel, of all things, with two chickens on his shoulder. I was somewhat excited as I spoke, "Sir, we have a large group of German prisoners in the house down the street, officers, non-coms and a large group of German G.I.s."

Do you know what this worthy example of a perfect, proper colonel said to me, in answer to my message of glad tidings He said, "Soldier, where is your rifle?"

I looked at him, astonished! *Gott in Himmel! Another schlemiel!*

"Sir," I responded, sheepishly, pointing toward the house. He nodded. I then saluted him again, turned, and ran back to the house. I told Sergeant Witt that the colonel was now aware of the situation here. When the colonel arrived with his men, we turned the prisoners over to him, German guns and all. Of all things, the great Lieutenant Burrito came out of the shadows, and with a forthright command took over our group, with orders to return to the houses we had left behind to pick up our equipment. We ran back to the houses, hoping to find everything still there. When we got there, down the cellar we went and found all was there under the mattresses. We put our equipment on, grabbed our rifles; then went up the stairs and out the door to the street, none the worse for wear, except that we were hungry. A harrowing experience though, never to be forgotten. Luck was with us—this time.

When we were all assembled, El Burrito gave the order to move out down the street in single file on both sides, to the end of the road out of town, heading for Cologne. There was no resistance to our movement forward from the Germans. We made a few of our usual forays into the villages off the main road, picking up a few German GI stragglers here and there, gladly offering to surrender, coming toward us with their hands held high. On coming to the outskirts of Cologne, we observed a peculiar sight off the road on both sides. There, standing up waist-high from their underground burrows, men, women, and children, like groundhogs, were staring at us as if we were creatures from outer space. Russian or Polish slaves of the master race?

As we moved into Cologne, we were told to check the interiors of buildings, which appeared to be empty. As we approached an overhead railroad alongside, we entered half shattered apartment houses to find rooms completely empty of any furnishings. However, when we descended to the basements, we found some occupants who had taken refuge from the bombings on the railroad overhead. They seemed to have found accommodations there of sorts, setting up cooking facilities and sleeping quarters, all by candlelight. We did not bother with them. Instead we looked into storage bins where we found trunks laden with household accessories of all types; chinaware, utensils, pillows, linen, clothing, bric-a-brac, etc. We left without a word. What price Aryan superiority had! We should all think of it!

Finally, we entered the center of Cologne, near the Rhine, without incident. We were settled in some empty buildings along the river. We heard that some units had caught the Germans unaware, and had managed to capture the bridge at Remagen, but we were not involved with that. Our shattered division was placed in reserve for reconstruction, rehabilitation, rest, and good hot food.

We did have small duties of checking the buildings in various sectors around our station. The next day, I was placed in a squad of some eight men, in charge of a corporal. We went off along a few side streets and alleys, checking empty rooms and basements. There was one incident that occurred that really enraged me. A German civilian was beating the hell out of a shabbily dressed male worker, or more like a servant or slave with a cut piece of garden hose. What is there about beating dogs or people with a garden hose?

I went up to the German, pointed the butt of my rifle about one inch from his mouth, and shouted in as much a mixture of my German accented Yiddish and English as I could muster, that I was going to cram the butt down his throat if he didn't stop beating the man, either Russian or Polish. Both the German and the victim stared at me, astonished! The victim collected himself, and took off. I told the German that the American military was now running the city, and that if I caught him again beating anyone else, I would turn him over to the military authorities, who would most likely put him to work cleaning and washing garbage cans.

That done, I walked away feeling that I had done my good boy scout duty of the day. I was once a boy scout in my younger days. When we got back to our quarters, we stepped into the yard where a dressing down, disciplinary harangue, was being set forth by El Burrito, alongside of whom was Sergeant Witt. It seemed that some of these idiotic characters had been molesting the German *haufraus* who had taken refuge in the basement of the buildings. I wouldn't touch them with a ten-foot pole. Fraternization was off limits, as we were lectured many times. We had enough to do than to molest German women. Only an idiot would try to entice a German woman—nothing to rave about—to *Shlafen gehen*. This, I found, to be a terrific scene to photograph. Which I did, I still have the photo.

The next day, I was called upon to perform another duty. The first sergeant, Ginelli, asked me to accompany a G.I. to a room on the upper floor, where I entered to find a couple of military doctors and some German women standing alongside a bed. A young girl, perhaps about twelve years of age, was lying in the bed, partially covered with a quilt. She appeared to be asleep, but I suspected she was dead. The doctors asked me to put some questions to the mother as to the child's age, cause of her condition, number of days of illness, food and water intake, symptoms before, etc., etc. I thought I had acquitted myself quite well, not that I was such a maven on such things. The doctors were satisfied. They had examined the deceased before I arrived. I had no idea what determination was made as to the cause of death. I was dismissed. I saluted and left the room.

When I returned to my room, I was told by my roommate to see Sergeant Ginelli. He gave me glad tidings. It was then that he informed me that I was granted a six-day pass to Paris; to be packed and ready at 0900, etc., etc. So, my ruminations were more or less at an end as we entered Rheims, France, late afternoon.

IX
Rheims and Paris

On arrival at the U.S. Rest and Rehabilitation Center at Rheims, we were assigned our bunks for the night, and given some orientation with the facilities and operations of the center. First, we were shown to the shower room, where I soaped myself several times just to get rid of the feeling of the muck, mire, and sweat that clung to me, and also shampoo of the head which I repeated several times. Then a large fresh towel, and when dry, I went to the wash basin and shaved.

Feeling fully and refreshingly washed up, we lined up for the issuance of newly laundered clothing—overcoat, jacket, shirt and trousers, long johns, socks, and new boots if needed. I would have liked a haircut, but there was no time for that. When all was done, dressed, we went down for dinner, buffet style. We picked up a tray and plastic plates, which we had laid out with beef stew, potatoes, green vegetables, bread and coffee. After which came a choice of desserts of various kinds. All in all, we felt, it was a much deserved banquet.

We went up to our bunks. We had a good cigarette, and off to bed. In the morning, we were up at 0730, down for breakfast with plenty to eat; a choice of eggs, ham, bacon, sausages, beans, grits, potatoes, toast and coffee. Then off to Paris. We all felt good after the previous night's rehabilitation and a good night's sleep. I felt relaxed, and happily anticipated spending time in that great city, renowned for its great achievements in the arts, music, literature, fashion, and gaiety. I looked forward to just visit the various sections of the city where the artists of all types of the nineteenth and twentieth centuries lived, and places they frequented. But first, I had to locate and get to the town where my younger brother was headquartered with his outfit as a driver for the trucks for the Red Ball Express.

I left my thoughts of the past rest and recede as I felt it best to approach Paris with a free and open mind. It was the present, and being alive to enjoy it was all that mattered now, I didn't realize how different it would be.

When we arrived in Paris in late afternoon, the driver checked in at a U.S.A. headquarters and information center. One of the cadre, boarded out truck and led the driver to the hotel where we were to be quartered for the next few nights. As we approached the hotel, we noticed a large marquee with large letters inscribed, attached to the balcony on the first floor, namely, *Hotel Londres et New York.* It was a welcome sight, a bit of home.

It looked and sounded good, but we were mistaken. The streets around the hotel were heaped in conical fashion, with wet, filthy slop, broken furniture, crockery, and smelly garbage. The truck stopped in front of the entrance to the hotel. We jumped off the truck, grabbed our duffel bags, and entered into a dark, musty, dismal lobby. We approached the "reception desk," entered our names and outfit, and were turned over to a Corporal (bellhop of sorts, but we carried our own "luggage"). The elevator didn't work, so we walked to the third floor, luggage on our shoulders. I was given the first room, which I entered off the hallway, in an apartment that consisted of two additional rooms in the back. A cot was placed alongside of a wall to the left of the entrance. There were no doors to any of the rooms. When I entered, I heard the conversations of other soldiers in the back rooms. The first thing I noticed was what appeared as an open toilet stall alongside of the cot—no seat cover.

I took off my overcoat and jacket, which I hung up on some hooks on one of the walls. I placed the duffel bag behind the head of the cot along the wall. That stall intrigued me. *My God,* I thought, *how could a toilet stall be placed alongside of a sleeping cot?* Well, as the saying goes, "This was *Paree.*" The French had their own thoughts on dealing with biological necessities.

Well, what to do? I had to relieve myself. So in my utter naïvete, I unbuttoned myself, took out my phallus, and proceeded to urinate into the stall. When finished, I buttoned up and looking about for a means to flush the stall, I noticed a foot pedal on the side. I pressed the pedal with my right foot.

"Holy Moses!" I exclaimed, as a geyser like jet of water suddenly shot up narrowly missing my nose by about two inches.

The soldiers in the back room came to the side doorway of my room, and laughingly explained, "Soldier, don't you know that you're in a cathouse? That stall is a *bidet* that the prostitutes use after quickie sessions with pick-ups off the streets. The water closet is down the hall."

I was utterly embarrassed. What could one expect of a naïve, inexperienced Jewish boy from Brownsville, Brooklyn, New York? As far as I knew, Jewish people from Eastern Europe were not privy to such vaginal hygienic practices. As for me, my experience in these matters was unabashedly none at all. Mark one more for experience. I was slowly getting there.

That completed, I was ready to enjoy the evening. We were previously told by the corporal that food and entertainment would be available at the Grand Hotel. The fellows in the back rooms came out and invited me and the others to join them on getting to the Grand Hotel. Walking through the dark, dismal streets of Paris was not exactly inviting, but since we were all going and meeting other soldiers on the way, it all made the walk spirited. When we got to the Grand Hotel—I had been checking the street signs and directions all the way—the lights were on inside, the band was in full swing, men and French girls were dancing in full swing also. Spirits were all aglow, and flowing. In the dining hall, food and drinks were laid out in buffet-style. What else could one ask for? Breakfast, lunch, and dinner, and facilities were always available.

There was a USA information desk in the hotel. I asked for information on getting to a certain town (I can't recall the name) where my brother was stationed with the Red Ball Express. They checked their maps, and the town was located. They then wrote out the directions on paper, the road and direction out of the city was indicated, ten miles out, for which I thanked them.

The next day, after breakfast, with many questions put to two autobus conductors, I was let off at the road that would take me out of town. I used the usual gesture (the thumb) for a lift from passing USA vehicles. In time, a US army jeep took me on that was going my way. A short time later, we got to the village I was seeking. I got off, thanked the driver, and walked about asking villagers for the headquarters of my brother's outfit. A good citizen took me there, where I was informed that his outfit had been transferred to Germany. Well, that was that! My conscience was cleared.

I finally managed to get a lift back to the city's main center near the Grand Hotel. There, I entered the dining hall, had some lunch, used the facilities, and decided to walk about for some shopping. I came across a parfumerie, and decided to send my wife some authentic Parisian perfume of which I was distressedly ignorant. I had to depend on the saleslady. I had a few dollars, and decided to put it to good use (who knew). I entered the store, and after some preliminary questions as to my wishes, the young female sales clerk took me over to a counter on which was placed a row of sample perfumes. After sniffing the aroma of these samples, I decided on

Bellodgia. I paid ten dollars for four ounces (I was told it was a good buy), and had it packed for mailing. I took it to the USA Post Office, and mailed it. That was another matter I had to take care of. At least, when she received it, she would know that I was still alive—in Paris.

For the couple of days I would spend in Paris, I wandered about the city, visiting some of the sections frequented and lived in by the artists of the nineteenth and twentieth centuries. One in particular, famous for its renown, for the sins of Sodom and Gomorrah, euphemistically called Pig Alley, for Place Pigalle, just below the Sacre Coeur. On my own, I went on a walking sightseeing tour of Paris as well, with my trusty 630 Box Camera. I recall walking along the Champs Elysées and taking photos of the very large poster of the film *Snow White and the Seven Dwarfs* as I passed by the cinema. I did not go into any of the cinemas. There were other interesting sections to go through. But my mood was depressed. I felt nothing but the drab, depressing atmosphere of cold, damp, cloudy weather, and dirty streets, nothing like the pictures once painted of Gay Paree. Well, what could one expect, considering the effects of war and the occupation of Paris by the Germans—a common repetition of human history.

But there was one element of gaiety that could not be diminished among the Gallic people, and that was as entertainers, with the spirit of joy, hope and love. How they showered their love on the American soldier—suffused with money, hunger for love, and animal heat. How all was gay in the ballroom of the Grand Hotel where the feel of closely held bodies among the dancers was the Elixir of Love. A much needed lift for both body and spirit. Don't get me wrong. I am not critical or prudish. I was all for the soldiers. Get whatever joy you can. Tomorrow, who knows?

There was one other place where gaiety was embraced—especially in the night. As I was wont to walk through the streets from my hotel quarters toward the Grand Hotel, in the darkness of night, a silhouette of a female body would whisper through the shadows of a doorway, plaintively, softly, *Couchez-moi, couchez-moi,* ("Sleep with me, sleep with me"), a cry for help. I was profoundly moved, but I could not respond in any meaningful way, as tempting as it may be. My mind was clouded with concerns of life, well-being, and conscience of faith. Who knows what would await anyone, upstairs in the darkened rooms. Better to let it go.

I never had any moral feeling of the waywardness of women. For thousands of years, throughout the ages of wars, plagues, natural upheavals, rape, social repression and exploitation, women have always found themselves on the outside, left out, on the bottom, neglected, demeaned, the most to suffer—classed among the disadvantaged, left to mourn the loss of their lovers, husbands, and sons—easy pickens, as one would say. Civilizations and life itself have paid a terrible price for the propagation of the thinking, practice, and exploitation of women throughout the ages to the present date, especially among the young.

As I walked on through the streets each night, just as I got to the other side, a bus, loaded with angels of the night, would come around the corner, recklessly leaning on two wheels, screeched along my side. The women with heads and shoulders waving scantily covered boobies, leaning out of the windows, waving handkerchiefs and scarves, shouting, *"Couchee, couchee,"* into the night. I recalled Eddie Cantor on stage singing the songs of "Couchee, Couchee," in memory of World War I. It hadn't changed much.

X

The Advance

When our time was up, we had reason to hurry back to Cologne. We heard that the Army had crossed the Rhine. We had every reason to believe that our outfit was involved.

On the way back, there was no overnight stay. We stopped only for reasons of necessity. I dozed a lot in spite of those rickety slats I was sitting on. For some reason I could not fathom, my box camera which I placed alongside of me slid off the seat, and rattled off the truck onto the road, bouncing about for several feet. I think I was half-asleep, which hindered my reflexes. I made a vain attempt to stop it from going off, but it didn't help. Too bad. I felt I had lost a good friend.

When we entered Cologne, we found that our outfit had already crossed the Rhine without casualties in spite of the repeated shelling by the Germans along a road front.

When we arrived at our outfit's C.P., Sergeant Ginelli called me to his office, welcomed me, and said he had an offer for me.

"Hanish," he began, "I am considering you for promotion to a staff sergeant's rating. We have a few openings for Staff Sergeant, and in view of your experience and your ability, which you have shown, to lead men, I think I am making a proper choice to fill the rank. If you have any reason to turn it down, please tell me. I will respect your decision."

This was unexpected, and I deeply appreciated it, but I did not want it.

"With all due respect, Sergeant," I replied, "After eight months of combat, I feel bushed, tired, and need all of my strength to keep myself going. To take charge of a squad of men, most of whom are replacements, about whom I knew nothing, I feel would be very stressful. I have no way of knowing if they would trust my leadership, nor would I find the trust in them necessary to follow my instructions or my commands."

This explanation was only part of my refusal. Something had happened to the whole complex of my inner feelings, like a dark, depressing cloud that enshrouds heavily on one's psyche. The episodes of denigration, disappointments, spiteful deprivations, bordering on humiliation, and the appraisal of my abilities as of no consequence, could not in any way be righted by any subsequent recognition of my ability to handle the requirements of a Staff Sergeant's rank. Not to mention the experience I had of seeing and feeling how some officers lead their men into combat from behind, instead of in the front, with a threatening gun jabbed into their backs. Not to mention the times when I saw men running off the field, muttering to themselves about not fighting and dying for those goddamn Jews.

Of course, Sergeant Ginelli knew nothing of all this, nor did I have any intention of reciting it all to him. He was one of the best and finest first sergeants I have ever had in service, humane, friendly, sympathetic, a human being if ever could be found. I could never thank him enough. I owe my survival to him.

The following is a quote from the combat record of the First Battalion, 415 Regiment, 104th Timber Wolf Division:

The battalion moved in a truck convoy from Cologne early in the morning of March 22nd, crossed the Rhine at Konigswenter, and passed into the hilly Remagen Bridge head. After taking over positions from the 413 Regiment, the battalion did not have long to wait for action. About 21:30 hours on the twenty-third of March, A and B Companies jumped from Eudenbach, Able reached its objective, meeting small arms fire for the most part, and the tea kettles (Tanks) moved up soon after. Baker, held down temporarily by machine gun fire, took Sassenberg. Meanwhile, B headquarters in Eudenbach became familiar with screaming meemies coming in, and the whack of the 155s going out. Tanks began to move out of the Remagen bridge head area, and the colossal breakthrough had begun.

For the next few weeks the infantry was mobile, following the Third Armored, breaking down spotty resistance, smashing counter attacks, paralyzing the Wehrmacht. The Wolves made a leap from Eudenbach in the bridge head and landed deep in the heart of Europe.

Penetrating deep in the heart of the Axis was hardly easy going. The advance of the U.S. Army moved on a broad front with several Infantry Divisions, armored artillery units and air force support. German counter attacks were often, and had to be repulsed. German defensive positions had to be naturalized. Many German prisoners were taken.

This ends the extent of the quote.

Coming back to my more personal experiences, which I found more interesting, we moved rapidly from town to town. On the way, we noticed small huts on the sides of the road just before entering a village. We were overtaken by a strong aroma of bacon being smoked, issuing forth from these huts. On opening the doors, we found chunks of bacon hanging from the roofs. So we came into possession of chunks of smoked bacon, which we cut down, and carried with us into the approaching village.

On entering the first farm house from which a mouth watering aroma of frying bacon was issuing forth, we found a room full of G.I.s, attending a large number of frying pans—gathered from neighboring farm houses—on which a multiple number of sunnyside eggs were place over slices of smoked, sizzling bacon. There were also two large pots of coffee brewing. Occupants of the house, as well as others from the other houses, were seated on the side next to this very large heated stove. Mostly elderly women were smiling, benignly, reposed.

The question arose, "Where do we get the eggs?" Why, of course, the answer came, "Out in the chicken coops in the yard." We walked out to the backyard, and the chickens were roosting in their coop. We took off our helmets, and without a by-your-leave, pushed the chickens aside, and picked up whatever eggs we could find, and filled our helmets. I picked four eggs. I realized later that I should have picked a few extra and had them hard-boiled so that I could carry them. A genuine, fresh, hard-boiled egg was a priceless commodity.

Back into the kitchen, I shared a frying pan with two others. We had our bacon, which was sliced and put into the hot pan. The aroma of bacon frying almost brought on hallucinations of reclining in Nirvana amidst a bevy of the most voluptuous, sweet smelling aphrodites, reclining like those pictured in Ingres' painting of the Harem lesbians and all.

Down to reality. I cut a good slab of bacon for myself, put it into the hot frying pan, and as the bacon began to sizzle, I cracked the shell of my eggs, and spilled them sunny-side up over the bacon. It is difficult to convey the ecstasy of frying fresh eggs and bacon, a very usual and ordinary chore at home in the States, but in a foreign country under combat conditions, subsisting on canned K-rations and c-rations, and only occasionally, on mushy beef stew, and the inevitable pork chops with a ring of inedible fat, desiccated mashed potatoes and beans, it was a meal of indescribable delight and satisfaction.

Just as I finished the frying, the captain and other officers came into the room, evidently attracted by the aroma of the frying bacon and eggs, and asked if we could get them some eggs. I was joined by two others, and we brought back enough eggs to feed an army. They thanked us, and proceeded to their own cooking. I stepped to the side, and partook of my own meal, after which I walked outside and rested up against the side of the house. I took out a cigarette, lit up, and when I inhaled my first puff, I felt a sense of peace coming over my body. All's well that ends well; a momentary illusory feeling.

A couple of hours of respite, and off we walked as usual. We finally arrived at a fairly large town in mid-afternoon where we were to quarter for the night. As we walked along the streets, we heard a large speaker, mounted on a truck, announcing to the inhabitants that they had to turn their cameras in at the Burgermeister's (Mayor's) office. They should be tagged with name and address for return in the future. When we finally settled in one of the unoccupied houses, Sergeant Witt approached me, and told me that the captain asked him to get some cameras for him and the other officers. The sergeant came to me to join him.

As we walked toward the Burgermeister's, we decided to borrow a flat deck shopping cart, on passing, with four small wheels, which had a large shaft extending with handle for pulling. On the way, a young girl came out of a house, carrying a small *35-mm* camera, placing herself just in front of us, hurrying like the little rabbit in *Alice in Wonderland,* muttering to herself. I caught up to her, stopped her, and asked where she was going. Of course, to the Burgermeister's to turn in her camera. I asked her if I could look at the camera. *Yes.*

I noticed that it was a *35mm* folding camera with a Zeiss 3.5 lens and range finder, excellent, just what I could surely use. I did lose my box camera on my return from Paris. I told her that I would take it to the Burgermeister's for her. She protested. I took out a sheet of writing paper from my pack, and wrote receipt for the camera for her to hold. I signed it John Doe. She was not too happy about it. I assured her it would be all right. I was lying through my teeth. Perhaps it was not right, but I didn't give a damn. I knew quite well that if I didn't take it, somebody else would; just as we were doing now for the captain. I remember too well how I was frisked by the German soldiers when I was captured.

Das ist der Krieg, Joe!

When we got to the Burgermeister's, and entered the office, by gosh, by golly! We found a room in which was stacked a pyramid of cameras of all sizes from *35mm* to 8×10 graphics. A bounty to behold! I couldn't get over this. I dreamed of owning a halfway decent camera which I could not afford to buy for years. And here it was for the taking. I was overtaken with unabashed greed, I must confess. Over the years, I had developed a knowledge of different types of cameras and their individual features. Sergeant Witt looked to me for advice, and he gathered a few for himself.

I had one camera already. I took a two-and-one-quarter Duo-reflex, a Welbilt, not as good as a Rolleiflex, which I could not find. Also a two-and-one-quarter, three-and-one-quarter folding camera with a Zeiss 3.5 lens; another *35mm* Voigtlander, and hooked into my belt on the back. I put the first aid kit in my backpack, and placed the *35mm,* I picked up from the girl in the street, into the pouch, which fitted perfectly. I did my best to pocket what cameras would fit, and those that didn't, I shoved under my jacket above the cord belt I used to tighten it. I certainly could carry them. I decided to pack two of the heaviest ones in a box to give the Mess Sergeant to hold for me. I would give him a camera for his trouble. I decided to take a chance. In the end, I never did see them again for some lame excuse like American prisoners ransacking the mess trucks. So, I forgot it. I had three good cameras. I had no remorse. As things turned out, the *35mm* was there to help me build a goodly photo record of the last few weeks of our stay in Germany.

Sergeant Witt, having made his pick, put them in his backpack, and we proceeded to load the cart with different types and sizes of cameras. We covered the cart with a table cover, and headed for the C.P. When we arrived there, the officers dived in to examine and hold for themselves. We left it all for them and walked out.

The next day we were off again, walking in single file on both sides of the highway as we left to win. After about a mile or two, we came across a horrible sight. We came up to a smoldering German army truck that had been hit with machine gun fire from Allied planes. The bullets evidently set the running truck on fire, causing it to explode, and blowing its occupants off on to the highway. There were two horribly burnt bodies near the rear of the truck, facing us, that was a twisted, smoldering wreck. The bodies were hardly recognizable as humans. The legs were missing, and the cut femur bones were protruding from the thighs. As we moved alongside of the bodies, we noticed that their faces were almost burnt to a crisp. One could only shudder at the sight, but we walked on without muttering a word. What price is glory?

As we continued on, word came down the line that President Roosevelt had died. This notice saddened us all. Our Commander-in-Chief, the greatest of them all, was dead. What now?

Further on, we came to an open clearing on the right side of the road. The entire outfit deviated off the road onto the field where we noticed some buildings set inland. As we approached them we noticed alongside a stockpile of empty rocket casings. When we entered the buildings, we found that it covered an underground factory for buzz bombs and rockets. We were told there were about nine to eleven levels down. The room we entered had long tables, chairs alongside, and clothing hooks on which some work clothes were hanging, along the walls. In time, we were told that this had been a slave labor underground plant, difficult to bomb from the air. A few of the men chanced walking down to the lower levels. I was not interested. We then took time out for a repast—with K-rations of course. Nothing like them. I never got the GIs from any of them.

At this time, I must interject descriptive writings from the Combat Record of the First Battalion 415th Regiment. To sum them up, they describe the undertakings of the various companies of the Regiment to force the German troops out of the defensive strongholds in the villages and towns, with successful thrusts, but not without cost in dead and casualties. We all surmised, that the ultimate goal of the first Army under General Bradley was Bitterfeld, one of the main industrial and chemical factories of Germany. Our outfit was lucky in that we were only involved in minimum confrontations. The others made it easier for us.

But we were to have an unexpected fatal incident for which there was no cause.

As we moved on, our company, or regiment, perhaps, was given the usual tasks of detailing small groups of men to check and to search small towns and villages alongside of the highways. As we were passing through a small town, what was left of my platoon, Company A., was detailed to check a German soldier's compound located in an open field at the edge of town.

Lieutenant El Burrito and his tall radio man, carrying a heavy casing of electronics and batteries for communication on his shoulders, Sergeant Witt, and twelve riflemen, which included me, came to this open field. We noticed a group of small buildings a short distance way to our left. At this point, the Lieutenant told Sergeant Witt to take the men to check on those buildings. He and radio man would return to the center of town to check on a few other things. They both turned and headed back to town. I must mention that the town was the most peaceful area in all of Germany. U.S. soldiers were moving about with young German girls, hands and arms, lovingly interlocked . . . so much for fraternization . . . smiling and talking gaily, as if they were tourists on vacation. No fault in that.

We headed for the buildings, walking over small mounds and depressions, a drainage ditch stretched a long way across our path, and a group of baled hay stacked two by two at right angles. As we approached the buildings, we noticed an entrance path to the compound that led in from the main road. The compound was fenced around with high, spear-shaped iron bars, over an extended number of feet.

At the entrance, Sergeant Witt suggested we walk in across an open, large courtyard opposite the buildings. Somehow, shivers crawled up my spine. Stored memories and those little gremlins that hover about our mind at times, warned me that this was not the thing to do. I expressed my fears to Sergeant Witt, who gave some credence to them. He said to me, "You and Blinski (that's what his name sounded like to me. I did not know him) stay here and wait for the Lieutenant, we're going around to the other entrance (which we noticed as we walked along the field), where we will enter the compound from there."

With that, he turned, took off to the left with ten of the men, and moved along the iron fence, behind which stood clumps of tall trees, around until they were no longer in sight. As I said before, I did not know this Blinski. He was someone new, a Repot-Depot, who joined us as we moved along the highways. Somehow his name sounded Polish to me. I did not think he was Jewish . . . as if it mattered.

As we stood there, we spoke and smoked, quite leisurely. I asked him about places of training, etc., etc., small talk. Then, suddenly, unexpectedly, it happened! As we spoke, perfectly relaxed, gun fire opened up at us from the three-story building on our right, and bullets sizzled past over head our helmets. We took off in a panic, and headed for those baled haystacks about fifty feet to our left, a fatal mistake. Somehow, I always felt that we should have gone along the iron fence which curved around in an arc to our left. But the suddenness of it left it more to our instinct than to our thought. As we ran, I bent low as I usually do, and called to Blinski, who was taller, to do likewise. I noticed that he was running straight up. I always felt it was better to get shot in the ass, than through the chest or head. The bullets kept coming.

As we approached the haystack, I performed a baseball slide, belly-whop (a second base one), into the baled hay area. As I went down, I heard Blinski utter a sound, "Ugh!" I knew he was hit. I maneuvered myself around to face him from behind the haystack. He was stretched out, face and chest to the ground.

I called, "Blinski, Blinski!" No reply. My heart was pounding to beat the band. I crawled over to him, grabbed his right arm to turn him halfway up so that I could see his face. Blood was flowing from his mouth. That was it! Those bastards! There was no reason for this. The war was about over! A victim of Teutonic Barbarism!

I wriggled my way back behind the haystack, uprighted myself to a sitting position with my back against the haystack. What to do? I fumbled in my jacket pocket for a cigarette with trembling hands, and finally lit up. I somehow became aware, in all this emotional upheaval, that there were gunshots and bursting mortar shells, sounds that were drifting from the area where Sergeant Witt and the others must have entered the compound. I began to feel vindicated in warning Sergeant Witt not to proceed into the open area of the compound. I think they would have picked us off, one by one. There was a better chance that they would have found cover on entering the other way, which they did.

I was beginning to calm down. It made more sense to return to the center of town since there obviously was a military C.P. (Where the hell was the Lieutenant). I could alert the officer in charge of what was going on here, and ask for assistance. That was it!

Alongside of the haystack, there was that narrow drainage ditch cutting across the field that extended from the town. I decided to crawl along in the ditch for cover. It really wasn't necessary, I found out later. I attached my rifle to my back with the rifle strap, moved into the ditch, and proceeded to crawl along toward town. Right there again, I met muck and mire, with an added smell of stinking garbage to keep me company. I caught up to a small culvert that led the drainage to run under the pathway, that ran from the main road to the other entrance of the compound. I crawled out of the ditch to the left, climbed up the slope of the pathway, and turned leftward toward town. No doubt I was glazed with the slop of muck and mire and smelled as well. Where the hell was the Lieutenant?

As I walked through the town in my quest for the military C.P., I accosted some GIs with my inquiry. They took one astonished stare at me, backed up, and pointed that-a-way to a small house down the street to the right. The military C.P. was plainly emblazoned—in no way to be missed. I walked up three steps, opened the door, and entered.

On my left, I entered a room in which was seated an officer, writing. I walked in, saluted the officer; a colonel (with the two chickens on his shoulders). He looked up, "Yes-s-s. What can I do for you, soldier" I could see that he was also staring at my woeful appearance, astonishingly.

I described the predicament our patrol was in. He thought for a moment. As if he had a long beard, like the sages of old, who used to stroke it in pondering a very important decision of state.

"Well," he replied, with all the profundity of a Solomon, "This is a matter for the infantry. We are artillery. Let me have your outfit, name, number, and other particulars regarding your company, regiment, and etc. I'll get in touch with them. In the meantime, you can go in to the next room, the kitchen, and dry your clothes near the hot stove."

"Yes, Sir. Thank you, Sir," I replied, as I saluted him, and walked into the next room.

There was a warm stove going, all right. I brought up a chair close to the stove, and lit up a cigarette. I wasn't even offered tea or coffee. I didn't know whether to cry, or burst out laughing. This colonel was a joke. Sergeant Witt and the guys, for all I knew, were being blasted to hell with gunfire and mortar shells, and the colonel, being a military officer with his soldiers milling around in the streets holding hands and arms with young, enticing German girls *schlafen gehen,* could only think of contacting my main outfit. By the time he contacted my outfit headquarters, wherever it might be, it would be all over, dead or alive. Who could tell! I quote:

Now, landsmen all, whoever you may be,
If you want to rise to the top of the tree,
If your soul isn't fettered to an office stool,
Be careful to be guided by this Golden Rule,
Stick close to your desk, and never go to sea,
And you all may be rulers of the Queen's Navee.
—G&S—*HMS Pinafore* VI

Ten minutes of thinking and drying was enough. I began to feel like a deserter. I decided to go back to the guys and add whatever support I could give them. I took off, by your leave, without a word to the colonel. I walked down the steps, and of course, I ran into Lieutenant El Burrito and his radio man as they were about to ascend the steps.

El Burrito looked at me, stared, and exclaimed, "What the hell are you doing here!"

I stared back. I was tempted to reply, "What the hell are *you* doing here!" but I thought otherwise. A wise thought. I kept my cool.

As we proceeded toward the open field, I related the whole story of what had occurred; of my experience with Blinski, and of Sergeant Witt and the guys under siege in the compound. I had come for help without avail. The Lieutenant said nothing. We came to the open field, and headed for the haystack. The noise of combat was still drifting from the compound.

When we got there, Blinski's body was still as I left it. The Lieutenant turned him over, took a small writing pad and pen, and made note of the name, serial number, and other points of reference, from the dog tags. He then turned the body back. He took Blinski's blanket, which was laid over the belt on the back, and covered the body completely. Then he took the bayonet from the scabbard and stabbed the blanket about four inches from the head to set it. The Lieutenant picked up Blinski's rifle, and we walked toward the entrance to the compound where the others had gone. As we moved in, the shooting suddenly stopped, and the stillness seemed unreal for a moment.

We walked along the pathway leading into the compound. There were a variety of small buildings and storage shacks on both sides of the road. Sergeant Witt and the ground must have had good coverage. A little way further in, we came across a long house on our left resembling a military barrack. As we approached the wooden steps leading up to the entrance, we heard Germans talking inside. When we ascended to the porch, and looked in through the open doors, we saw three German army nurses, and men, probably wounded, lying in beds parallel to each other, heads up to the sides of the walls, on both sides of the aisle.

They stopped talking and stared at us. We stopped at the doorway, and we stared at them. They stared at us. We stared at them. They stared at us. We stared at them. Enough staring already! The lieutenant turned and headed down the steps. We followed.

We started to walk toward the building from which came the rifle shots at Blinski and me. As we came nearer to the building, we heard singing wafting in the air from thence. Incredulous! What the hell was that? The words of the song penetrated our ears, hardly sonorous.

You are my sunshine,
My only sunshine,
You make me happy,
When skies are gray,
You will never know dear,
How much I love you,
Please don't take my love away.

The other night dear as I lay sleeping
I dreamed I held you in my arms
When I awoke dear, I was mistaken,
And I hung my head and cried.

You are my sunshine
My only sunshine
  (reprise)

When we got to the open door of the building, we saw a sight, unbelievable! Sergeant Witt, with an open bottle of beer in his right hand, and his left arm over the shoulder of a German officer, whose left arm encircled Sergeant Witt's neck, and in his right hand also holding an open bottle of beer. They were both singing the song and swaying laterally.

On their left, a couple of GIs were similarly embraced with a German non-com, all holding open bottles of beer. Behind in the dark, the rest of the GIs (no casualties) were seated on a table with two German privates (I presumed), each one with an open bottle of beer in their hands, drinking as they continued to sing, "You are my sunshine, etc., etc." There were a couple of half-empty cartons of unopened bottles of beer in front of them.

No doubt, they were all slightly inebriated. I should say drunk, but this was an auspicious occasion. They all survived, and managed to capture the Germans. Can't blame them for celebrating. The lieutenant and I stood there, nonplussed for a moment. I walked up to the swaying Sergeant Witt, and exclaimed, "Sergeant, those bastards just killed Blinski!"

The sergeant looked at me almost incomprehensively, and replied, "Well, too bad. Have a drink of beer, and you too, Lieutenant."

I was in no mood for beer, and neither was the lieutenant, who waited for an other five minutes before speaking up, "OK, Sergeant Witt and you men, enough is enough! Gather up their arms, and lead them out as prisoners! This is an order. I have had enough of this nonsense!"

As ordered, the German's arms were picked up, and the officers' and non-coms' pistols were taken, and they were led out with their hands up. We proceeded into town, much to the amazement of the soldiers and civilians there, and joined up with the battalion somewhere out of town. The prisoners were turned over to it, and the lieutenant submitted Blinski's name and serial number as killed in action. The whereabouts of his body was also indicated.

To recapitulate, according to the Battalion Combat Manual,

After moving out of the Remagen bridge head area, the colossal break-through had begun. For the next few weeks, the infantry was mobile, fol-lowing the Third Armored, breaking down spotty resistance, smashing counterattacks, paralyzing the Wehrmacht. This whole campaign was car-ried out by various units of the Division, Battalion Regiments, and Com-panies. The town of Medebach lies on the route to Bitterfeld. Able Company, attached to the Second Battalion was sent on a special mission to Unselen, and the rest of Baker Company was sent to Medelin.

The purpose of citing the Combat manual was to indicate that my small outfit was part of a massive military movement to smash the German Wehrmacht and to take as many prisoners as possible.

During the end of March and beginning of April 1945, the Germans unleashed furious counterattacks on our attempts to advance, causing many casualties among us, but causing twice as many of them as we re-sisted. Many German prisoners were taken. There was no doubt that the German Army was bleeding profusely.

The Manual again: "On April Third, the Battalion was relieved by the Seventh Armored, and assembled at Usselin. The Battalion then moved to Willingin, and another race began, which paused momentarily at the Weser River. During this period, the First Battalion was doing more than its share to keep the German soldiers in the Ruhr pocket from escaping. You would never learn of this in reading all those books of the campaigns on the Western Front by those self-appointed analysts, like Stephen Ambrose. Not one of his books mention the contribution of the 104th Divi-sion under General Terry Allen toward the defeat of the German Wehrmacht.

"When the final figures were tabulated, more jerries had been trapped in the pocket than even the most optimistic estimate had approached. In the light of these figures, holding at Wedebach and Asselin was an operation of first class military importance. The First Battalion held fast."

On the road to Bitterfeld, many German towns were taken, most with-out resistance, and some with considerable artillery and gunfire. They were quickly overcome. In one town, however, we were hit with artillery fire that landed in the midst of town, shattering glass windows, and demol-ishing some homes. Imagine, the German military were bombing their own towns and villages, still occupied by civilians, especially elderly women and children. In one instance, under shellfire, we ran down the

168

basement of a house where we found elderly women crammed in. As the explosives outside rent the air, one elderly woman remarked (I hope my German is correct), *"Gott hat uns bestrafen, for Juden hat uns schlecht behandeln."* The expression struck me as follows, "God is punishing us for the way we mistreated the Jews."

I honored this old lady. I could only imagine that she must have had Jewish friends and neighbors. I found later on that the old generation of Germans, especially the women, many of whom lost husbands, perhaps grandfathers, sons and grandchildren, that were left with nothing but grief and loneliness, lack of food, and perhaps, shelter—nothing but sad memories of the past life, which had lost its meaning.

As we approached Bitterfeld, preparations were made for attack on the city. Bitterfeld, as mentioned before was an important industrial city on the Mulde River, center of I.G. Farben Industry and gas manufacturing plants. Because of the danger that poisonous gases might be released during the attack, gas masks were distributed and checked by everyone.

Once more, the manual:

Under cover of darkness of April Nineteenth, A and B Companies moved into the factories outside of Holzweisig to join Company C. At 0130 on April Twentieth, Able and Baker with supporting machine gunfire, sections from DOG, crept into positions on the line of departure to await the attack. After witnessing an intensive artillery preparation, the companies moved stealthfully toward Holzweissig—outskirts of Bitterfeld. The Germans were surprised in their positions and taken prisoner. The attacking forces infiltrated deeply into Holzweissig and elements of A, B, D Companies continued penetrating the town. During the day, Charlie (C) company joined the push against resistance, consisting of gun fire, panzer thrusts, and mortar fire. The Battalion completed the capture of the town, moving up to the overpass and railroad yard that separated Holzweissig from Bitterfeld. The following day the Battalion moved into Bitterfeld.

When my outfit, as little as it was, walked into Bitterfeld, we came upon a group of GIs and German prisoners arranged in a circle. The Germans were the Home Guard, about six men, consisting of two youngsters (16–17), and four very old men, probably in their late seventies or early eighties, wearing uniforms of WWI vintage. The old men were smiling with one tooth showing. The young men appeared sullen and quiet. In the middle, on the ground were all kinds of pieces of junk, normally carried in men's pockets. It seemed that the GIs had ordered the Germans to empty their pockets. This is the usual practice in taking prisoners. The first thing is to empty their pockets, naturally, of course!

There was nothing there to consider. So we walked on through the city to the end, and started on the road to Halle. After several miles of hard walking, we were bushed. We arrived in Halle about nightfall, and quartered in whatever empty house we could find. There was sporadic gunfire, going on about the town, but we were not affected.

In one of the rooms, I slumped down against a wall, took out a K-ration, cut open the can, turned it over in the palm of my left hand, and found I had a piece of cheese with brown bits of bacon, enmeshed. I savored the bite of it, with some hard tack, I chewed away, almost dozing off, and with a swig of water from the canteen, I pictured myself sitting at a café outdoor table, watching the passing parade of strollers in one of those narrow streets of Paris in spring time.

Just as I was about finished with half of the cheese, I was rudely brought out of my reverie by the lieutenant, who tapped me on my shoulder and said, "The Battalion driver outside can't locate Blinski's body and asked for someone to guide him."

So, that was it. I was the one to go with him. I wrapped the rest of the cheese and hard tack in my handkerchief, put it in my jacket pocket, grabbed my rifle, and walked out into the street. A jeep was waiting with the driver. I hopped on, and off we went into the cold, dark air, without a word.

The driver drove into Bitterfeld, and stopped at the Battalion C.P. We got out, and entered a room lit by army lamps. I was told to take a seat, be at ease, and relax for the rest of the night. I sat down on a wall bench, which placed me on the side of along table. I took out the rest of the cheese and hard tack from my pocket, unwrapped the handkerchief, and began to chew away. I kept looking at a pile of small cardboard cartons, with excited amazement, labeled *35mm,* black and white Agfa film, thirty-six frames each. Of course, the city was the place where Agfa film works was located. My mind was alerted and my eyes were riveted on more cartons. I was trying to figure several ways of getting my hands on at least one carton. Of course, you could always ask. Just as I was about to ask, a major came through the doorway opposite me, noticed my staring eyes, and said, "Help yourself."

By golly! I was greedy enough to want to take as much as I could carry. That was impossible. There were ten cartridges to a carton. I took one carton, and placed it in my haversack. Well, the trip was worth going. I had film for my *35mm* liberated camera. I took the camera from my back pouch, and loaded it with a roll of film. After, I dozed off.

I was awakened by the driver in the morning. First, I had to relieve myself. No breakfast. Then, again I hopped on the jeep. My conversation with the driver consisted of his concern on locating the body. I did my best to describe the location. When we arrived at the town, I directed him to proceed through it to the open field. I saw the haystack and pointed it out to the driver. He drove over the mounds and troughs of the field, negotiated the drainage ditch, and stopped alongside the haystack. Blinski's body laid there untouched, the blanket still covering him.

We pulled out the bayonet, and uncovered the body. My reaction on seeing his face was emotional, but I restrained it. The driver lifted the body at the shoulders and I took the legs. As we carried it to the jeep, I began to realize the meaning of dead weight. The weight of the body seemed to increase two or three times its normal. We laid the body on the back seat, and covered it with the blanket after putting the bayonet in its scabbard on Blinski's belt.

"Next, to the graves registration unit," the driver said. I leaned back in the seat, took a pack of cigarettes out of my pocket, offered one to the driver, which he took, and we both lit up. There was nothing to talk about, each of us locked in our thoughts, I imagine, of life and death. I leaped into vagaries of thought on the fickleness of life in this unsettled era. This was the second time I was called upon to carry a dead soldier off the field.

When we came to the graves registration unit, I know not where, we drove into the yard next to the building, stopped, and entered the room where a sergeant and three of his assistants were seated around a large table. On the table were the remains of an open ten-in-one ration carton. Alongside of that was a half-consumed, very large can of marmalade, two cut round loaves of white bread, a slab of butter, and cups of coffee. All of which was consumed with a ravishing appetite.

We told them we had a body in our jeep outside. As they all got up, they invited us to partake of the food on the table. The driver sat down at the table, and proceeded to cut for himself a slice of bread. He spread some butter on it, ladled out a large spoonful of jam, and smeared it out on the bread. It was not for me. My stomach was in no condition for this. When they brought the body in, and laid it alongside of five other bodies, my stomach certainly was in no mood for bread and jam in spite of the fact that I had nothing to eat all morning. I walked outside, and slumped up against the wall of the building in the bright, warm sunshine. I lit a cigarette.

The month was April, spring time—a beginning, birds were flying about the bare branches of the trees, and chirping the joys of life. A woman with her two children, who were prancing alongside of her on the sidewalk, were gleefully sounding off. U.S. Army jeeps and trucks were scurrying by on the highway. The springtime air, cool and fresh, brought promise of joy and hope of being alive. But not on the inside among the fallen dead. A wasted death! *Fini! Terminado! Enden!* What did it all lead to Nothing! *De rien! De nada!* They were born to live and die before their time!

One thinks back to events in WWI. Eric Remarque wrote a novel about German students urged on by glowing words of honor, heroism, of dying for the glory of the Fatherland, pride of the greatest accomplishment and worth to be achieved on the field of battle; urged on with emotion and evangelical exuberance by their instructor. Half of the class joyfully joined immediately, and in the end, as each one met their doom and loss of sight and limb, they found that in the end, there was nothing but disillusionment and misery.

Have things changed over the years? Hardly!

In Flanders fields the poppies blow,
Between the crosses row on row,
That mark our place, and in the sky
The larks, still bravely singing, fly
Scarce heard amid the guns below
We are the dead. Short days ago
We lived, felt down, saw sunset glow,
Loved, and were loved, and now we lie
In Flanders field.

Take up our quarrel with the foe;
To you, from failing hands we throw
The torch; be yours to hold it high.
If you break faith with us who die
We shall not sleep, though poppies grow
In Flanders field.

—John McCrae

(Reply)

We took up the torch, but in efforts vain,
Amidst the cannon's roar, death did sow
Bodies, whose youth was given to remain
In Flanders field among the crosses row on row.

For Honor and Glory, our efforts expended,
Amidst the battle fray; our bodies laid low.
We too loved life, saw 'sunset glow,'
Felt love befriended,
Now we too shall lie along those
Long since laid in peace and repose,
In Flanders Fields, where the poppies blow,
Between the crosses, row on row.

They were born but to live,
With joy of youth, and of love,
In their prime
But as fate chose not life to give
For wanton 'delusions from above,'
They were born to die before their time.

—A.H.

Then again, I can think of nought but the poets.

—John Donne

Any man's death diminishes me
Because I am involved with Mankind.
And, therefore, never send to know for
Whom the Bell Tolls; it tolls for Thee.

—Thomas Gray

The Boast of Heraldry
The Pomp of Power
And all that Beauty, all that wealth ere gave
Awaits alike the inevitable hour,
The paths of glory lead but to the grave.

    The driver came out and took his seat on the jeep. I got up and joined him in the adjoining seat. Nothing was said, as we rode back to Halle. I found it difficult to shake off the depressed mood I had of my experience there.

    When we arrived in Halle, the streets were astir. Jeeps were moving on the main road from anywhere, some carrying Hitler Jungen (twelve to fifteen years of age) in uniform, seated on the front hoods. They were the ones who were firing on the troops in the darkness of night. I didn't hear of any casualties.

From Halle, we were put on trucks, and taken to the Nordhausen Concentration Camp, where we parked outside. We knew nothing of this notorious death camp. As a matter of fact, of any death camps. We were kept in abysmal ignorance. Only the officers went into the camp, and when they came out, nothing was said. Had we been permitted to go in, I would have taken photos as a witness. Later, we found out about the condition of the Jewish inmates there, and what had happened to them in the camp. It was incomprehensible to contemplate that this could occur in a civilized, Christian world today. Where was God?!

We went onto Bitterfeld, where we were relieved by the Ninth Division. We continued on to Dachau, where the Battalion set up its C.P. and quarters in a feudal castle with its knights in armor, and ancestral portraits. This was in East Germany, Prussia. I remember walking through the hallways of the cold and somber castle as we examined each knight armor, previously worn by its former occupants of the Middle Ages, the gallant Prussian knights of old. They must have had some interesting history to tell.

Again the Manual, the Record of the 415th Regt.:

Able Company occupied two small farming communities, Lubshutz and Dognitz; Baker went to Deuben, and Charlie to Koisey.

Hunting deer in the woods was a popular sport in the area. Venison steak was a delicious addition to the limited rations issued during this period. I remember a fallen deer being carried back to our quarters on a pole. The venison steaks were out of this world. This hunting was forbidden by headquarters on complaints of the German civilians, who claimed that they were being deprived of their own source of food. Hunting weapons included light machine guns, carbine, and M1s (hand grenades were also used). Able Company pushed a notorious Nazi out of his position as mayor of Lubshutz, and helped materially in the return of self-government to the town.

The most memorable of this period was the trip made to the Elbe River to contact the Russians. A few days prior to the cessation of hostilities, two missions left Dachau early one morning, I took photos of this set

174

up, taking different routes, which led to the river. The first mission, well armed, and prepared even to the medics in case of some resistance along the way, policed its sector of No-Man's Land. This stretch of country had never been penetrated by either the Russians nor the Americans. The first mission contacted the Russians eight miles south of Torgau, while the second met the Russians on the banks of the river opposite Torgau. This latter place was the assembly point for the whole celebration. We were informed by our officers that the Americans were not permitted to go over the river into the Russian zone. The Russians came over to the Timberwolves, in force, however, and brought vodka, picture-taking apparatus—I had my own—and hearty greetings. Shutters snapped, weapons were exchanged and demonstrated, and the Russian WAC representation did their best to make the Americans welcome. A fine time was had by all!

The war with Germany came to an end while the Battalion was situated in these positions. It was a great relief knowing that the last attack had been made in Germany, that the last foxhole had been hacked out of the German soil. I was ecstatic! I had committed myself well, and had survived.

For the purposes of patrol duty, the Battalion moved once again, this time in the vicinity of Köthen.

It was at this time that the lieutenant, Burrito, as we checked apartment dwellings on the way, met and became overwhelmed by a very attractive, sexually inviting middle-aged German woman, whose husband, an SS man at that, had been killed in Russia. Thank God for that. She, being alone, except for elderly mother, found herself, *etwas,* with a scarcity of food and other needs, was amenable to the Lieutenant's swan song for companionship and a bit, who knows, maybe a lot of *schlafen gehen* (couchee, couchee, for all that).

Somehow, he managed to have her tag along with us as we went from town to town. He appointed me his aide-de-camp to proceed ahead to make sure to obtain sleeping quarters for himself and his *fraulein.* He made use of my ability to communicate with the *hausfraus* for such accommodations. Of course, this was readily given, and of course, there will be the requisite gifts, and not money, either. Somehow, the ban on fraternization went by the wayside. This was quite acceptable and common from top to bottom.

The battalion units were split up to police various towns and villages. Able Company (mine) was placed in Frassdorf. Administrative profiles were made of each man's personnel file. A point system was set up and a total was tabulated for each one for discharge.

Fear that the division might be sent directly to the Pacific was dispelled, when the War Department declared that the 104th was to be deployed, but only after a period of furloughs and training in the States.

First, there were several things that occurred in the village worth mentioning as the administration was occupied with its problems.

Sleeping quarters had to be rationed out, as it were, in private homes, run by hausfraus, no men about. Of course, the Army took it upon itself to furnish the Germans with food and condiments. Within a short time, there seemed hardly enough for the hausfraus who initiated a campaign called *schlafen gehen.* For a little extra of their virtue, a soldier could obtain their endearing embraces. *Oy!* How could anyone go for that with such as they. Each day, it was common to find these women in their worn housedresses, unkept hair, middle-aged, entering our quarters, offering their intimate wares for a bar of chocolate, a fruit bar, candy, whatever—*schlafen gehen!*

It was during our stay in this village, that one day it was announced that there would be a ceremony for the awarding of medals for meritorious service in combat. Sergeant Ginelli had recommended me for that medal. I had only to write up a significant incident in which I had shown unusual initiative in accomplishing a successful end. I had no trouble with this since there were several that I could have chosen, with a little artistic license.

With others, as we lined up in the village square, I was awarded the bronze star and with that three battle stars for participating in three major campaigns which, luckily, I survived.

We had two hot meals a day, a K-ration for lunch. It didn't take long before we began to notice that there was a short supply of sugar, salt, coffee, canned milk, and other seasonings on the dining room table. I took it upon myself (such *chutzpah*) to go up to the Mess Sergeant's quarters to confront him with this sad tale of our deprivation, which we felt was unbearable. I walked up one flight of steps, knocked on the Sergeant's door, and without waiting for an invitation to come in, I foolishly walked in.

There, the Sergeant was seated, and on his lap, facing me, was an adorable looking blonde Mädchen (perhaps eighteen or nineteen years of age), her arms entwined around his neck, lovingly kissing his cheeks. The Sergeant's left hand was up her "poop," and his right hand was seeking out her bare breasts, behind an opened front blouse, as expressions of ecstasy issued from her lips, between the kisses.

Holy Moses! I had unwittingly disturbed a hornet's sex hive, in full embrace. The Mädchen released her arms from the Sergeant's neck. He released his arms from wherever. The Sergeant then stared at me with flings of spears from his bulging eyes.

"What the hell do you want?" he growled.

I wasn't fazed. I have been growled at many times by frustrated Sergeants. I responded, meekly, "Sergeant, for some reason or other (I knew the reason), there seems to be a lack of sugar, coffee, tea, salt, etc. and etc."

His grumpy retort was quick enough. "Yeah! I'll take care of it. Now get the hell out of here!" *Schlafen gehen.*

I could see that is was quite indelicate of me to walk in at such a rapturous moment. "Right!" I said, and as I turned toward the door, they both burst out laughing. I opened the door, walked out to the stairwell, as I shut it, and descended a few steps, sat down, and vented a paroxysm of laughter. Nothing changed. The reason for the disappearance of those condiments from the dining table was quite obvious. But something had to be said. Needless to say, we raided the supply for available K-rations which also eventually disappeared. Hail to the victors!

There was another operation I became involved in. I made the acquaintance of another Jewish soldier working in battalion headquarters, named Benjamin. He approached me one day, and told me that he was informed to go over to battalion supply to obtain photographic apparatus and chemicals for photo processing. He asked me to join him. Of course! I hopped in his jeep and off we went. We gathered up everything we needed. He was more knowledgeable of the processing than I was.

We took over an empty house, and set up our trays and enlarging equipment in one of the rooms. We covered up the windows with heavy drapes to darken the room, and placed an orange bulb in the light socket. We strung cord across the room to hang our processed rolls of negatives.

We placed three trays on the table. The first tray was filled with developer, the second with stop bath, and the third with fixer, for the film, and after, for the processing of the exposed paper. The film was processed through the developer by holding the edges with the fingers of each hand, right and left, and moving it through the developer in a rocking motion. It was pulled out by inspection; then through the stop bath, and dropped into the fixer for about 10 mintues.

After the film was washed, they were hung individually with clamps on the stretched cord. The wetness was squeezed out by squeegee. When dried, we enlarged each frame by projection onto an easel for three-and-one-half by five prints.

We each processed our own film, and then took on those who submitted their film for processing—no distinction made for rank.

A general sense of peace and relaxation pervaded the atmosphere in the village. Squads of men were sent through the streets of the village to patrol the areas, and to help in policing them. Others found ways of enjoying their stay. Just for a few weeks of this, and then to move out for return to the States. When the time came to move out we walked through the streets in single file on both sides. The women of the village were lined along, and waved us goodbye with tears in their eyes. They knew they were to be faced with an uncertain future. East Germany was also tied to the Russians.

Once again to the manual:

From the vicinity of Halle, the Battalion boarded trucks on June 13, to travel to the trains at Leipzig. The first leg of the long train trip home was to begin. For the purposes of the record, the last towns the battalion occupied were: Headquarters and Dog, Guttenburg Charlie and Baker, Seaben; and Able, Sennewitz.

It was the forty and eights again that transported the homeward bound troops, the slow train passed through cities of Germany that were not familiar, Weimar, Jena, Gotha, Frankfurt-on-Main, Mainz, etc. And then the train rolled through the Maginot Line, into France. After detraining in the Le Havre area, the Cigarette Circuit began. First, it was Camp Lucky Strike, and a week later, Herbert Tarryton.

On July first, the battalions boarded the SS *John Erickson* at Le Havre, along with about two others and experienced the trials of double loading. On the second, the ship sailed, and on the eleventh, the Erickson landed at Staten Island. Home again! What a relief to be in God's Country once more!

XI

Discharged

The trip to Le Havre, France was on the long, slow train in the forty and eight's, a narrow gauge railway with narrow box cars. We were stuffed into the cars like forty men and eight horses, which gave the cars their names. Straw was spread over the floor and sprayed with DDT. Our beds were made. We hopped on, and were sprayed with DDT powder, almost choking us. The use of DDT was later discontinued years later because it was found to be detrimental to the survival of animals in the forests. So much for our safety.

As the train moved slowly along the tracks, there were several things we could do to accommodate ourselves. Several men would take turns to sit at the edge of the sliding door platform which was kept open. A wooden bar was stretched from side to side, and four men would sit at the edge, feet dangling, and arms around the wooden bar.

Inside, men would stretch out for a nap. Some would write their letters, and others would clear away the straw and play cards. The train would stop occasionally for us to get off and, to relieve ourselves—wherever. Also there were stops to have our meals, some hot, some K-rationed, and that was that.

I took a lot of photos on the way—of the men, and of the destruction to towns and railway stations along the way. We boarded the ship at Le Havre, and sailed to the U.S.A.

From Staten Island, we were taken to Camp Kilmer, New Jersey, where thirty-day furlough passes were issued. While the furloughs were in progress, dramatic world events changed the whole course of civilization. The war and the future of every Timberwolf. The atom bomb, and the end of the war with Japan climaxed the whole series of happenings, which for the division, began when the 104th started home.

It was in the month of October that the 104th settled at Camp San Luis Obispo. My wife managed to travel by train and bus to San Luis Obispo. I picked her up at the bus stop in town.

We found a room to border for our stay at a single family home at Yokum's Tract, somewhere off the center of town. The couple which took us in were very friendly and did their best to make us comfortable.

San Luis Obispo laid astride the main highway from Los Angeles to San Francisco. It had a reputation for fine bathing at Pismo Beach. The camp was set up alongside of the beach, which made swimming easy for the men. Each morning, weekdays, I would be up, and to start off for the shuttle bus station in the center of town, to grab the bus to the camp.

The walk to the town each morning was very pleasant. We had no rain during our two week stay. The sidewalks were sparsely covered with fallen walnuts from the trees alongside, which I picked up, cracked, and ate the contents. Along the way, there were gardens that stretched out from the small, attractive homes set down slightly below the sidewalk. They were filled with patches of vegetable and tubrous plants, fully ripe. I was overwhelmed by the atmosphere of peace, warmth, and friendliness of the people in town. It was a far cry from what I witnessed in Europe.

On weekends, we walked about town. We were invited in by an elderly couple Swiss who saw us admiring their grapes, hanging from their makeshift trellis. We partook of a bunch of very sweet green grapes, offered to each of us. We did some swimming at the beach, and then on the last weekend we took an excursion by bus to Paso Robles, which was having a festival of sorts. There was a parade down the main street in which men from our division participated. I took some photos.

On October 27, 1945, I received my discharge papers, honorable, of course, and thus was free at last. My wife's brother, who had been working in San Francisco Naval station as a sheet metal worker, and his wife, came by with their car to pick us up in San Luis Obispo, and we all set forth for Los Angeles to meet their uncle.

From Los Angeles I had to travel by train to take us back to New York City. We stopped on the way at Salt Lake City for a two-day visit, and then on to New York City by way of Chicago.

And so ends my saga of my experiences in the U.S. Army and in combat that covered a period of three years and three months. Like so many others who went through the same experience in combat, I was never the same.

Epilogue

As with most soldiers discharged from military service, my feeling of freedom was greater than any other that one can experience. Freedom in a democracy is more precious than any other dreamed up Utopias, by erstwhile progenitors, divine and otherwise, who sternly promulgate from on High—down, instead of listening to the voices of those from the Foggy Bottom, seeking relief from the burdens of dealing with the material realities of survival, and the havoc wrought by nature.

Looking back through history, the human animal is constantly confronted with vagaries of an inconstant world of earthly disasters, and those of its own human frailties; it has sought the powers of conceptual divinities in a transcendental universe to which were added anthropomorphic traits. This concept has led to metaphoric description of revelations in thought and in feeling that can only be accepted on faith. There is no end to the growth of faiths, all contending of being the one and only truly divine, conceived through God's favor.

As mankind struggled along the path of history, with its head above the hazy clouds, occasionally looking down at its feet which laboriously struggled through the *shlop* of natural and human disasters, battered and humbled, it was awakened only to the revelation of this reality. So mankind has set its course throughout time with the exuberance of such irrational consciousness that could very well lead to the barrenness of life, and of the future, exemplified in the red dust of the planet Mars.

The twentieth century was marked by the appearance of ideological sociocratic thinking previously hashed around by the social thinkers of the nineteenth century, which descended from the foggy haze of the upper regions, propounded by men, especially Marx, Engels, Lenin, and Hitler, whose reigns were immersed in the faulted mush of material dialectics. So was the half-baked thinking, universally adopted among the hare-brained intellectual *literati,* full of contradictions and inconsistencies, so apparent, but overlooked. This so influenced political megalomaniacs to burst forth irrationally on military adventures, and the execution of millions of people for not meeting their established tenets of thought, color, race, and faith.

No civilization could survive the physical destruction of towns, villages, and cities, irresponsible mayhem, the shredding of spiritual and material values, the loss of family cohesiveness, of love and caring, the loss of credibility in religious teaching and practice, the loss of life's meaning, caused by the horrific fratricidal military conflicts of WWI and WWII, and others.

The Holy Bible had divined that God is One, which on further examination could very well be a Revelation of Wisdom. It can also be said that the past, present, and future are also one, as well being attributes of God, for they are inextricably bound together in an evolving evolute, which reveals that as time progresses, both social and natural events seem to repeat themselves, giving the impression that change is progress toward a better life, though in reality it turns out to be illusory.

Someday, we may all sit down for a moment instead of flying off into cyberspace and the Internet, to try to define progress. Yes, there have been advances in medicine, science, food production, material betterment for some, but not for the millions and millions, living in the muck and mire of poverty, constantly aggravated by unmitigated sexual activity, eventually leading to an explosion of population growth of such horrific dimensions that we witness the massive movement of people shorn of material well-being and intellect that swept over Europe in the Middle Ages.

So extensive has this explosion been, that the exploitation of the Earth's resources necessary to sustain life has been greatly diminished. The growth of technology to meet the ever growing demand to enjoy the good life, that the quality of life has been corrupted and soiled by hucksters of crass materialism and crass commercialism of the publishers, the media, and the raucous, gut-spilling musician. If this were not enough, the air we struggle to breathe has been contaminated with the smoke emitted from fossil burning fuel, smog, and gasoline fumes, that we are already seeing people in some countries so befogged with smog, that they are forced to get around with air filtering masks. All this and at least to mention the spread of venereal diseases.

It is written in the Old Testament that Moses, after leading his people out of bondage from Egypt, roaming through the Sinai Desert, and coming unto the mount, where he ascended, upon God's bidding, to seek divine guidance to help him create a nation of people so that they may grow and live in peace, that would dispense justice and freedom for all, under God. So it was divinely inscribed, "I am the Lord thy God, thou shalt have no other gods before me."

When Moses descended from the mount, and saw the people dancing around the golden calf in worship, and forswearing the oath they made to follow the commandments of God, Moses, in a fit of rage, smashed the tablets against the rocks and melted down the golden calf. Needless to say that Moses was recalled by God and given a new set of inscribed tablets.

The Israelites recoiled in fear, and promised once again to obey the Commandments of God. Throughout the centuries, the Jews had held onto these Mosaic Codes to which they owe their lives, and for which they have died. Other religious faiths saw fit to throw them out the windows of their houses of worship.

"I am the Lord thy God," saith the commandment, "thou shalt have no other gods before me." And yet, throughout the centuries and up to the present, prominent men and women, and those successful in achievement and financial beneficence, are honored and raised to divine stature, with attributes of lesser gods, albeit with feet of clay. Politician, actors, sports people, as well as wrestlers, basketball players, baseball players, inspired writers and hucksters, amassing millions by purveying tripe, mushed up hope, and miracles are held in such high esteem of sagacity, foresight, mesmerizing beatitude, that they are chosen to help us ascend to the heavens of eternal bliss and health. Unfortunately, as with Icarus, son of Daedalus, they and those of the worshiping crowds, have wings that are fashioned in wax.

One of the most calamitous acts of perfidy perpetuated on a people whose doctrines of faith served to enhance the growth of others, have done nothing more than diminish their credibility. The monstrous acts of destruction of millions of a faith abjured for its divinely inspired reverence to their very souls, held without quarter, infuriatingly stubborn in its practice, and intolerable in its indifference to change.

Throughout time, man has attempted to understand the nature of God, which has metaphorically unwrapped itself in a veil of reflective material so as to make man see himself in his own image, as reflected in that of God. It would seem that in this reflection of his own image, God is addressing man to find his own solutions in the search for the good life, and that man would act with rational consciousness, he may yet find his way into the Kingdom of God, where peace and everlasting life would be enshrined. There is no way out for mankind but to look to itself, and not to the heavens above.

As mankind trudges painfully along the paths to the everlasting invisible beyond, it finds itself in a world of its own making. It is ever thus, through:

Der Muck and der mire,
Der Schleppin' and Der Schloppin',
Der Scheissen and Der Bombin,
Der Angst and Der Weepin'
Oy Vay iz uns!
Alles Kaput!

Let Us Pray!

Ah, make the most of what we yet may spend
Before we too into The Dust descend,
Dust unto Dust, and under Dust to be
Sans Wine, Sans Song, Sans Singer, and Sans End.

With them the seed of Wisdom did I sow,
And with mine own hand wrought to make it grow,
And this was all the harvest that I reap'd,
I came like Water, and like Wind I go.

The Moving Finger writes, and having writ
Moves on: nor will all your Piety nor Wit
Shall lure it back to cancel half a line
Nor all your Tears wash out a word of it.

—The Rubaiyat of Omar Khayyam

—Edward Fitzgerald